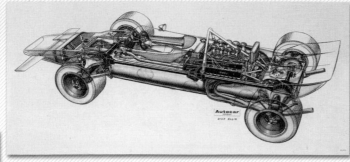

1974 GRAND PRIX OF THE UNITED STATES
WATKINS GLEN, NEW YORK, U.S.A. — OCTOBER 6

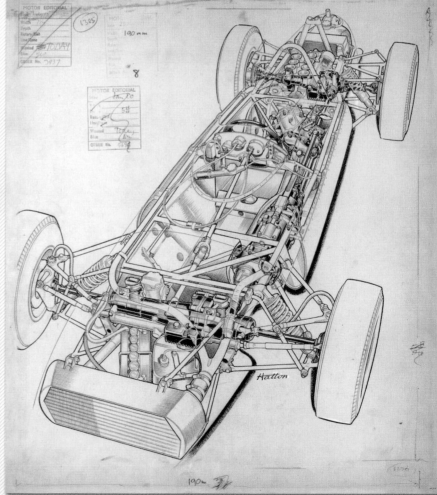

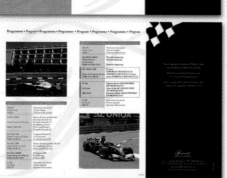

THE TREASURES OF
FORMULA ONE

IN ASSOCIATION WITH **THE DONINGTON GRAND PRIX COLLECTION**

SECOND EDITION

BRUCE JONES

CARLTON
BOOKS

CONTENTS

FOREWORD BY SIR STIRLING MOSS, O.B.E.

Whether you follow Formula One through its drivers, its teams or simply season by season, this book will be your guide as it charts the course from the first road races at the end of the nineteenth century via the first grand prix in 1906 through to the modern day, covering the greatest stories alongside the endless technical developments, along with all the important milestones throughout its history. Read about how the World Championship was launched in 1950 and how the British "garagistes", as Enzo Ferrari would call them disparagingly, took on the establishment, turned the sport on its head and shaped the sport as we know it today. Find out how Lotus chief Colin Chapman took technology to new levels and how McLaren designer Adrian Newey did the same three decades later.

More than the stories, more than the facts, more than the stats, you'll find the connections in this book between circuits as markedly different as Silverstone, Monaco and Watkins Glen. You'll read about how Senna put on Formula One's greatest masterclass in the wet opening lap of the European GP at Donington Park in 1993 and have to balance that against my near fatal accident at Goodwood in 1962 … and see the flimsy-looking cork polo helmet I wore back in those days and used until I retired in June 2011. You'll also follow Ferrari's incredible journey from the 1920s to the current day as it rose from being one man's dream to a global brand, with success galore but quite a few setbacks along the way.

Throughout the book, you'll be able to marvel at the world-beating array of Formula One cars at the Donington Grand Prix Collection, as well as read about how Formula One is spreading around the planet, experimenting with night racing in Singapore, as it moves from its old European stamping ground. It's not all glory and beautiful machinery, though, as death was very much of the sport until the 1980s and there are sad stories such as the loss of young talent like Roger Williamson, Tom Pryce and the inimitable Gilles Villeneuve.

You'll also get the opportunity to hold history in your hands. In many places, you'll find pockets or slips or envelopes in which are placed facsimiles of many fascinating documents from Formula One history. From my Maserati and Vanwall drivers' contracts to race programmes from famous Grand Prix venues to curiosities such as the guest's brochure from the exclusive Fairmont Hotel, Monte Carlo, these one-of-a-kind items will leap from the pages of history – and this book – right into your fingers.

Formula One is a visual festival for hundreds of millions the world over, and now in this book, it's a tactile one for you, one that we hope that you will dip in and out of as you discover more and more elements of why it's the world's most spectacular sport.

BELOW: A panoramic photograph of the Nurburgring, taken in 1937.

nternationales Eifelrennen 1937 auf dem Nürburgring

10 Kautz
5 Müller
18 Rügen
Seeman
24 Carraroli
15 Soffietti
23 Graf Frietics
19 Balestrero
21 Mandi…la
FOTO-URBA
KOBLEN

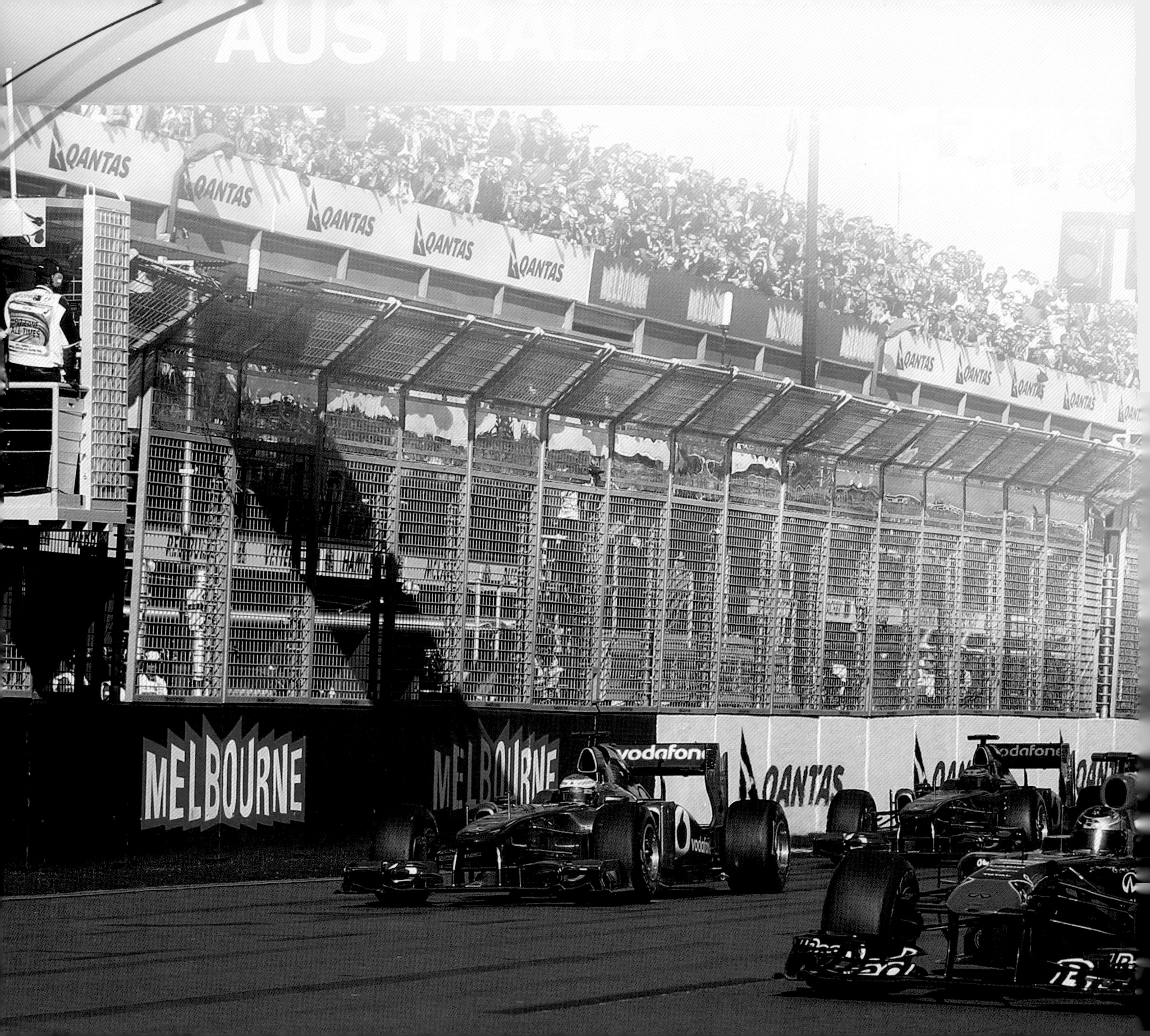
QANTAS
MELBOURNE
vodafone

INTRODUCTION

It was only natural that no sooner had the motorised vehicle been invented than it became something that needed to be raced. In the pioneering days of the 1890s, race entries were small, race distances long (on public roads) and those that witnessed them generally surprised.

However, as this book highlights, motor racing was quick to develop and hasn't stopped doing so since, with each of the intervening decades producing a host more technological innovations that have transformed the sport. From disc brakes to aerodynamic wings to turbocharged engines, the changes have kept on coming, making the cars ever faster. Indeed, many of the rules that have been introduced have been simply to keep the speed of the cars in check, in the interests of the safety of drivers and spectators alike.

One constant woven into the fabric of the sport is spectacle, as cars going fast around corners, preferably jostling for position, will never cease to entertain. Throw in other constants like noise and colour and it's little surprise that it makes for perfect television and is even better live to enjoy every factor of this eternally mesmerising mix.

Of course, the sport today as it contests 20 grands prix per season across the globe is a far cry from the World Championship's first decade, the 1950s, when there were as few as six events, all in Europe. Things were much simpler then, and much cheaper. Then the arrival in the 1960s of the widely available Ford Cosworth DFV engine led to a rapid expansion of teams at a time when the manufacturers' forces were dwindling. It changed the face of the sport as it spawned or made

competitive teams that later rose to the top, like Williams and McLaren, teams that would go on to challenge the team that continues to define Formula One: Ferrari.

In some ways, the World Championship is now a business as much as a sport, as the money involved is considerable. For example, teams used to employ as few as 20 staff. Now 20 times that is the norm, and Ferrari employs 900.

There's a tendency for young fans to say that the racing now is better than ever, and we're certainly enjoying a purple patch as Lewis Hamilton, Sebastian Vettel and Fernando Alonso scrap for glory. Yet, according to our age, we all have a favourite period, normally the one in which we first fell in love with F1, and The Treasures of Formula One offers a chance to compare and contrast the sport across the decades.

When gathering the letters, contracts, blueprint drawings, promotional posters and annotated race programmes to accompany the text, one thing became ever more apparent. This is that drivers now are like drivers at any point since that first road race between Paris and Rouen in 1894, as they simply want to get out onto the track and race. The money they earn now is stratospheric, but many would still do it even if they weren't paid a penny, as the buzz they get from it never diminishes. Just don't tell their agents.

Bruce Jones
September 2011

BELOW: In the shape of things to come in 2011, Red Bull Racing's Sebastian Vettel powers away from pole position in the first grand prix of the season, at Melbourne. He would go on to win the race and retain his world title.

1890s-1900s
PIONEERS OF MOTOR RACING

LEFT: Louis Renault formed the Renault car company in 1899 with his brothers Fernand and Marcel.

FAR LEFT: Marcel Renault started racing in 1900 but was killed in the 1903 Paris–Madrid road race.

The cars weren't very fast to start with, but the impact of the early races was considerable as the city-to-city races gave way to the first contests on closed courses.

Motor cars first appeared in the nineteenth century and it did not take long for men to want to see who could drive fastest. From this simple premise, manufacturers realized that if their cars were seen as the quickest, then more people would buy them. The first race, held on 22 July 1894 along a route of public roads running from Paris to Rouen, was organized by a Parisian newspaper, *Le Petit Journal*. The reaction was electric, the event made the headlines, and soon other races were being held, both in Europe and America, and a new sport was born, with hundreds of thousands of people lining the routes to take a look at these racing machines.

As if to prove that politics, rules and wrangling are nothing new, the winner of the first race, Jules de Dion, was not allowed to accept the prize purse as he'd driven solo, not carrying a riding mechanic, thus handing the prize to Georges Lemaitre. The average speed was just 11.58mph.

To many people along the route, this was the first time that they'd ever seen a car and there was considerable danger as people would walk out into the road to watch the car power away, unaware that another was following behind... Indeed, the death of a boy spectator on the 1901 Paris to Berlin race led to France banning racing until the French motor industry pressed for it to be permitted again. A similar incident caused the

stoppage of the 1903 Bordeaux to Madrid race, when a car hit spectators doing just this. Thereafter, the French government insisted that roads had to be closed off for racing, with crowds kept back by barriers.

It wasn't just the crowd that needed protecting as the cars became ever faster. By 1903, for example, cars were averaging 65mph in some events, which is faster than it seems as the majority of roads were rough and rutted, with their loose surfaces being kicked up into dust clouds that compromised visibility. With our contemporary mind-set, we would have considered the safety of the drivers and their riding mechanics as well, but this never entered the minds of racers at the start of the twentieth century, for they were wrapped up in the excitement of racing and their attitudes to mortality were markedly different from ours. Health and safety was a topic that wouldn't be considered for half a century and more.

Not surprisingly, the first driver fatality wasn't long in coming, in 1898, on the Paris to Nice road race. It was a bizarre incident too, as one driver waved another through, and that overtaking driver, the Marquis de Montaignac, took his hand off the tiller to acknowledge the gesture and swerved into the other car, knocking it off the road and killing the riding mechanic. Turning to see what happened, the Marquis inverted his own car and died of his injuries.

These weren't the only deaths, but the move towards permanent circuits had begun, with the banked Brooklands circuit in Surrey the first to be opened in 1907. Here, unlike a city-to-city road race, the spectators could see the cars more than once; and unlike a road circuit, they could also see pretty much all of the circuit. The Americans weren't far behind, with banked ovals, often made from wood, being opened right across the country, with the jewel in its crown, the Indianapolis Motor Speedway, holding its first race in 1909.

From that very first race in 1894, the French had been predominant through the de Dion, Panhard, Mors and Renault marques, but the inaugural Gordon Bennett Trophy race in 1900 encouraged other nations to take part, with British, German and Italian entries soon starting to

ABOVE: Racing was soon worldwide, as shown by this de Dion 8hp waiting for the start in Melbourne in 1908.

LEFT: Léon Théry and his riding mechanic set off in their Richard-Brasier in the 1904 Gordon Bennett Cup race at Homburg in Germany.

ENCLOSURE: Promotional postcards at the start of the century , such as these for road races around Spa in Belgium, were wonderfully artistic. Copyright © Musée de la Ville d'Eaux, Spa, Belgium.

BELOW: Felice Nazarro entered the French GP in this Fiat in 1907 and came away victorious after nearly seven hours of racing at Dieppe.

BOTTOM: This Mercedes 60 from 1904 shows how exposed to the elements the driver and riding mechanic were.

challenge the French as national teams of three doing battle in the once-a-year competition. Created by the *New York Herald*'s European correspondent, James Gordon Bennett, this soon caught on, with Panhard winning the first two events before the British Napier marque triumphed in 1902. Mercedes took on and beat Panhard in 1903, with the ebullient Camille Jenatzy winning the event in Ireland. The following year, the French fought back with Léon Théry winning in Germany in a Richard-Brasier. This combination won again, in France, in 1905.

Then, in 1906, the first grand prix, French of course, was held on a route around public roads near Le Mans (see sidebar). Part of the reason for this was that the Gordon Bennett Trophy rules were restricting the number of manufacturers that could take part, and the French wanted more. The event was a success, and a road circuit near Dieppe was home to the French Grand Prix in 1907, with the Italians taking the glory as a Fiat won in the hands of Felice Nazarro, and again in 1908 when the German driver Christian Lautenschlager was victorious for Mercedes.

The Americans also put up their hands for a grand prix in 1908 and had to endure European cars taking a clean sweep of the top six positions at Savannah as Louis Wagner won for Fiat.

FRENCH GRAND PRIX 1906

The circuit for the first grand prix was 65 miles long, running around a triangular course of closed public roads east of the city of Le Mans. The event comprised one race on the Saturday and another on the Sunday. The 32 cars were sent off for six laps at 90-second intervals. Mercedes, Fiat and Itala entered three-car teams, with Mercedes tipped to set the pace. The French were confident, though, with 23 cars entered by Panhard, de Dietrich, Hotchkiss, Darracq and Renault. The Italians had six entries. The French confidence was well placed as Ferenc Szisz – former riding mechanic to Louis Renault – drove his Renault (below) to first place at the end of the first day and outright victory on the second, helped by using detachable wheel rims that sped up tyre changing. Albert Clément had been second at the end of the first race, but fell to third as Fiat's Felice Nazarro usurped him in the second race.

1910s-1920s
GETTING SERIOUS

The First World War brought Europe to a halt, but the evolution of the racing car that followed was remarkable as cars were made ever lighter, nimbler and faster.

The Americans started to get their act together in 1910 when David Bruce-Brown won the American Grand Prize in a Benz at Savannah, usurping foreign interlopers. He repeated the feat the following year in a Fiat at the same venue, and Fiat won again when the Grand Prize was held in Milwaukee in 1912, this time with Caleb Bragg driving. Emerging from an economic slump, there was a French Grand Prix again that year and Georges Boillot won that at Dieppe for Peugeot, as he did the next at Amiens in 1913.

The changing face of European racing was shown in 1914 when German racer Christian Lautenschlager won the French Grand Prix for Mercedes. The First World War then brought Europe to a halt for half a decade and racing also went into hibernation, with no grands prix from 1915 to 1920.

Once the depletion of a generation was over, racing returned in the 1920s bigger, better and more competitive than ever before, and it was at this point that the development of cars really took off, with a 3000cc maximum capacity introduced. By 1922, that engine capacity figure had been reduced to 2000cc and cars continued to be made lighter and nimbler, ever distancing themselves from the huge cars with unlimited engine capacity that had gone before, with cars sporting 18-litre aero engines not uncommon. The minimum weight of the cars used for grand prix racing was reduced from 800kg to 650kg.

Perhaps because the First World War hadn't knocked the stuffing out of the USA the way it had the European nations, it was the American Duesenberg driver Jimmy Murphy who won the first grand prix since

1914, the 1921 French Grand Prix at Le Mans, with fellow American Ralph de Palma second in a Ballot and French ace Jules Goux third, also in a Ballot. European honour was regained at the year's other top race, the Italian Grand Prix at Brescia, with victory going to Goux.

What was really happening at this point was that the American and European manufacturers were choosing different courses of development. The Americans were producing cars to perform on their banked ovals, whereas the European racers were made to handle road courses and thus were made lighter to ensure that they were nimble.

By 1922, the Americans could no longer match the Europeans and concentrated more on winning their own Indianapolis 500, and Felice Nazzaro won the French Grand Prix at Strasbourg – the first to have a massed start – in a Fiat, with Pietro Bordino taking the honours in Italy.

British marque Sunbeam entered a copy of the 1922 Fiat 804 in 1923 and won the French Grand Prix at Tours through Henry Segrave, then the Spanish Grand Prix at Sitges through Albert Divo, with Carlo Salamano winning the intervening race in a new Fiat.

The sport was propelled to a new level for 1924 with the introduction of the Alfa Romeo P2. Giuseppe Campari and Antonio Ascari won with it – with Ascari leading home an Alfa Romeo one-two-three-four result at Monza – before it went on to win the first World Championship for Manufacturers in 1925 in what was dubbed motor racing's Golden Age. For this season, cars had to have two seats, as before, but riding mechanics were outlawed. Indeed their requirement had already been reduced as race durations were cut. Ascari had won the opening round, but then was killed when he crashed in his home grand prix at Montlhéry. Twelve-cylinder Delages also bagged a couple of wins for the French.

For 1926, engine size was cut to 1500cc, and with Alfa Romeo pulling out as a worldwide economic slump hit hard, the pendulum swung to Bugatti which won four of the six grands prix. Meanwhile there were signs of Mercedes rising to the top thanks to Rudolf Caracciola (see sidebar) as the balance of power continued to shift.

ABOVE: Georges Boillot smiles in the cockpit of his Peugeot in 1912 before winning the French GP at Dieppe.

LEFT: Christian Lautenschlager's Mercedes GP kicks up the dust at Lyon en route to winning the 1914 French GP.

BELOW: A Dunlop Cord tyre from the 1920s mounted on a period wire wheel.

BOTTOM: Henry Segrave swerves his Sunbeam around the Duesenbergs of eventual winner Jimmy Murphy and André Dubonnet in the 1921 French GP.

Delage and Mercedes-Benz shared the honours in 1927, when cars ran in single-seater format for the first time, with Robert Benoist winning four grands prix for Delage, Otto Merz one for Mercedes-Benz.

In 1928, with the recession hitting ever harder, two of the five grands prix were run as sportscar events, with British driver "W. Williams" winning one at St Gaudens in France in a Bugatti and Caracciola the other at the Nurburgring in a Mercedes-Benz. When the grand prix racers were let loose, however, it was Bugatti all the way as Louis Chiron won the San Sebastian and Spanish Grands Prix at Lasarte and the Italian Grand Prix in his dainty T35C. He added two more wins at the German and Spanish Grands Prix, but only after "W. Williams" had won twice, also in a Bugatti, and then the intense yet charismatic Achille Varzi won the one that counted to Alfa Romeo, the Italian Grand Prix.

Overall, these were two troubled decades for motor sport, dominated by war and then economic depression and the Americans going their own way, but blessed with appreciable car evolution.

BELOW: Bugattis to the fore in the first Monaco GP in 1929, with eventual winner W. Williams (left) side by side with Philippe Etancelin.

BOTTOM MIDDLE: This 1921 Sunbeam 3-litre won the Tourist Trophy on the Isle of Man in the hands of Jean Chassagne.

BOTTOM RIGHT: The contents of the Pratts fuel cans may have been perfection, but pouring them into the cars was both messy and unsafe.

RUDOLF CARACCIOLA

Having pestered Mercedes-Benz to join its racing team, Rudolf was given his break in the mid-1920s and impressed in particular on hillclimbs. Bravery was required for these and this was something that the young German had in spadefuls. His breakthrough victory came in the 1926 German Grand Prix, when he was 25. It was wet that day at Avus and the skills he displayed there earned him the nickname Der Regenmeister (the rain master). He went on to win the German Grand Prix at the Nurburgring in 1928 when it was a sportscar race. Even when armed with a large car unsuitable for conditions, such as the Mercedes SSJKL that he used to finish third at Monaco in 1929 (below), he seemed able to make the car dance to his tune. Through the 1930s, in spite of shattering his right thigh at Monaco in 1933, Rudolf won the German Grand Prix four more times plus nine other grands prix and the Mille Miglia sportscar race.

MASERATI AND ALFA ROMEO

The battle between Alfa Romeo and Maserati to be the best Italian marque has ebbed and flowed since the 1920s, with each driving the other to ever greater heights.

Italian marques have always been among the most coveted. Maybe Fiat doesn't quite fit into that mould, but Maserati and Alfa Romeo manufactured not only beautiful-looking cars but ones that went seriously fast, and spent much of the 1930s and later the 1950s locked in combat. For many fans, you either supported the cloverleaf (Alfa Romeo's emblem) or the trident (Maserati).

Alfa Romeo was founded in 1909 and soon went racing, entering the grand prix arena in 1924, with its P2 racer an instant hit. The attack was for just two years before Alfa Romeo withdrew for financial reasons. Maserati was founded by the Maserati brothers in the early 1920s, and its first job was to build a straight-eight engine for the Diatto grand prix car. Its cars were experimental, running with twin engines, but success soon followed, with Achille Varzi taking a 26M to victory in the 1930 Monza Grand Prix, chased across the line by Luigi Arcangeli's sister car. He also won that year's Spanish Grand Prix.

Then Alfa Romeo raised the bar by introducing its 8C Monza for 1931, with Giuseppe Campari winning the 1931 Italian Grand Prix and Tazio Nuvolari leading an Alfa Romeo one-two at Monaco in 1932. Maserati

was unable to respond. Then, after being nationalized and handing over the reins of its team to Enzo Ferrari, Alfa Romeo pressed still harder and launched the Tipo B, also known as the P3, with Nuvolari winning on its first two outings before team-mate Rudolf Caracciola headed him home in the German Grand Prix. It employed two driveshafts, enabling the designer to bring the driver's seat down between them, lowering the centre of gravity, and when its fixed axle was replaced by independent suspension it handled even better, and Tazio Nuvolari would famously make it lap faster still by using its agility to use four-wheel drifts.

Maserati fought back with its 8CM in 1933, with Nuvolari, who had changed teams, winning the Belgian Grand Prix. But Alfa Romeo won five grands prix through Luigi Fagioli, Louis Chiron and Guy Moll into 1934 when their battle was overshadowed by the arrival of the German giants Auto Union and Mercedes-Benz, who scooped most of the laurels, apart from those for the 1935 German Grand Prix when Nuvolari drove like a giant to keep them at bay.

Proving that the automotive business was precarious, the Maserati brothers sold out to the Orsi family in 1937, but were kept on until 1947 on a management contract. At the same time, Alfa Romeo took control of its racing team again and Gioacchino Colombo designed the Tipo 158, but it was hidden in a cow-shed at the start of the Second World War. Maserati made the fast but fragile twin-supercharged 8CTF, and its highlight was third place in the German Grand Prix, giving the Germans a scare by leading for much of the race. The 8CTF also scored a rare foreign

ABOVE: Emmanuel de Graffenried made it two wins in two years for Maserati's 4CLT in the British GP when he was first home at Silverstone in 1949.

TOP: Kenelm Lee Guinness keeps his Sunbeam ahead of Antonio Ascari's Alfa Romeo P2 in the 1924 French GP, a race won by Alfa's Giuseppe Campari.

BELOW: Tazio Nuvolari won for both Alfa Romeo and Maserati. This is the Italian ace at speed in the 1933 Nice GP in a Maserati 8CM.

ALFA ROMEO P2

This beauty was launched in 1924, its twin-camshaft, supercharged, eight-cylinder engine and sleek bodywork designed by Vittorio Jano, with its drivers enjoying 145bhp at 5500rpm. The chassis was built on to two metal rails sitting on rigid axles over leaf springs. Victory first time out in the hands of Giuseppe Campari proved its worth as it set new standards. It also gave Alfa Romeo the chance to lord it over Fiat who'd been doing the winning until then. Its advantage was so great in winning the 1925 Belgian Grand Prix that Jano put on a lunch for his drivers, mid-race, while the mechanics polished the cars... This gave Jano special pleasure as he'd joined from Fiat in 1923. The P2s raced on until 1929, by which time they were producing 175bhp in their attempts to keep the Bugattis, Delages and Mercedes-Benz racers behind them, and Achille Varzi rounded out its career by winning the Italian Grand Prix.

success in the Indianapolis 500 in 1939 and 1940, driven by Wilbur Shaw.

After the war there was a series of minor races from 1945, but it wasn't until 1947 that grand prix racing got going again. The Maserati 4CLs had to make do with being second best when the Alfa Romeo 158s were recovered from their hiding place. There was no German opposition due to post-war reparations, but the Alfettas were untouchable through 1947, with Jean-Pierre Wimille leading their attack, until they skipped the French Grand Prix. This was also the year in which the Maserati brothers' management period expired and they started the OSCA racing car company, producing sports racing cars but also a few single-seaters that were raced ineffectually in Formula One.

Giuseppe Farina started 1948 well for Maserati by winning at Monaco, but the Alfettas came back and cleaned up until they skipped the British Grand Prix, which went to Maserati's Luigi Villoresi. This set the stage for a decade of domination by Italian machinery, with Ferrari joining in, albeit a decade interrupted in the mid-1950s by Mercedes-Benz's hugely successful two-year raid on the Formula One scene.

Before the World Championship began in 1950, Alfa Romeo took 1949 off, but hit the ground running, winning every round, including the final one when its 159 model arrived and triumphed first time out. Alfa racer Giuseppe Farina was crowned as the inaugural World Champion.

In 1951, the 159 was again the car to have. Ferrari pushed it increasingly hard, but could not prevent Juan Manuel Fangio becoming Alfa Romeo's second World Champion. Then, at the end of the season, Alfa Romeo shocked the sport by quitting Formula One. The marque would not appear again until 1979, after which it raced, without success, until 1985.

Maserati stayed on, however, and the introduction of the 2.5-litre engine rules for 1954 brought it back into the reckoning, with Fangio driving its 250F to victory in its first two outings on his way to his second world title. Mercedes-Benz won almost at will through until the end of 1955, but then withdrew, after which the 250F kept on setting the pace, Fangio taking his fifth and final world title in 1957. From here on, Italian glory on the grand prix scene would be the sole property of Ferrari.

ABOVE: Jean Behra holds off fellow Maserati 250F racer Juan Manuel Fangio for the second place in the early laps of the 1958 Argentinian GP.

RIGHT: The Alfa Romeo Bimotore is one of the stars of the Donington Collection, with two engines and 500bhp that was good for 200mph...

BELOW LEFT: Juan Manuel Fangio brought his 1951 title-winning season to a close by winning the Spanish GP at Pedralbes in this Alfa Romeo 159.

THE 1930s
ITALY AND GERMANY DOMINATE

Italian racing red was pushed aside in the late 1930s by the silver cars from Germany that propelled Grand Prix racing on to a whole new level of speed and power.

When the Second World War broke out in 1939, the motor racing map of Europe was already changing. The domination of Italian marques had given way to the technically adventurous and immaculately prepared German marques Auto Union and Mercedes-Benz.

After Bugatti and Maserati had shared the spoils in 1930, the races were lengthened to 10 hours in 1931, more than five times the maximum length of a current grand prix. Again Bugatti was the most successful marque, with Louis Chiron its leading driver, while Alfa Romeo and Mercedes-Benz played supporting roles. Thankfully, race duration was reduced by as much as half for 1932, with Tazio Nuvolari and Rudolf Caracciola starring in Alfa Romeo Tipo P3s, and then a 500km maximum was imposed for 1933, when Achille Varzi challenged in his Bugatti and Nuvolari made a successful switch to racing a Maserati 8CM.

There were still no restrictions on weight or engine size, however, so engineers could have a field day, and Alfa Romeo got it most right with its P3. A minimum weight of 750kg was enforced for 1934, but the most notable development was the arrival of Auto Union and Mercedes-Benz, both teams bankrolled by government backing to promote the National Socialist movement. It was clear that Alfa Romeo's dominance was coming to an end, as they couldn't match the newcomers' budgets. Italian racing red was going to give way to the silver of the German racers. The German racing colour had been white, but so ambitious were Auto Union and Mercedes-Benz that they entered their cars unpainted to save weight. And so the term Silver Arrows was coined for these high-tech racers.

Hans Stuck struck the first blow for Auto Union, in the German Grand Prix, and he won again in Switzerland, with plucky René Dreyfus winning for Bugatti at Spa-Francorchamps in between. Then, at Monza, Mercedes-Benz scored its breakthrough with Rudolf Caracciola partnered by Luigi Fagioli before Auto Union and Mercedes-Benz rounded out the year with another win apiece.

It was hardly surprising that no one else got a look-in in 1935, except at the German Grand Prix when Tazio Nuvolari produced one of the all-time top drives to beat them in his Alfa Romeo. He had just worked his way past Caracciola's Mercedes to lead when the leading quartet pitted. Manfred von Brauchitsch was the first to emerge, after a 47-second stop.

ABOVE: Leather skull caps were worn from the early days through until the early 1950s before helmets were introduced for safety reasons.

TOP: Auto Union and Mercedes took on the Italian marques in the mid-1930s and beat them. This is Hans Stuck's Auto Union heading to victory in the 1934 German GP at the Nurburgring.

MIDDLE RIGHT: Tazio Nuvolari struck back for Italy in 1935 by winning the German GP in this Alfa Romeo P3.

ABOVE: Winner Achille Varzi's Bugatti T51 and Baconin Borzacchini's Alfa Romeo 8C Monza fight for position at the start at Monaco in 1933.

RIGHT: The Donington Challenge Cup was awarded to the winner of the Donington Grand Prix from 1935 to 1938.

Nuvolari came out sixth after a broken fuel-pumping device took his stop out to two minutes 14 seconds. And so started his second charge. The 14-mile lap of the Nurburgring took close on 11 minutes, but the fact that he was second by the end of his out-lap says it all. That just left von Brauchitsch, who was 69 seconds to the good. The gap came down and down until von Brauchitsch, famously ragged and hard on tyres, pressed too hard and had a tyre failure on the final tour, leaving Nuvolari to a famous, fabulous win.

Mercedes-Benz ended 1935 holding the upper hand, and skipping the final two grands prix, but 1936 was Auto Union's year. Bernd Rosemeyer led the way once the 16-cylinder Type C Auto Union hit form, with increasing engine capacity stretching the German teams ever further ahead of the Italian marques. With their 6-litre (rear) engines Auto Union cleaned up, and Mercedes-Benz won only the opening race of the campaign, at Monaco.

Stung by this failure, Mercedes-Benz struck back in 1937 by launching its W125, a car that could finish only third on its debut in Belgium behind two Auto Unions, but then won in Monaco, Switzerland, Italy and Czechoslovakia before Auto Union took the season finale at Donington Park. Caracciola was the top driver, with three wins. Such was the W125s' power output, 646bhp, that this wouldn't be exceeded in any form of racing until 1965 when a supercharged Novi-Ferguson entered for the Indianapolis 500 pushed out 775bhp. Sundry Formula One rule changes protected this record, but the level of engineering in the best of the 1930s racers was sky-high.

ABOVE: Manfred von Brauchitsch at speed in his Mercedes-Benz W154 in the 1938 German Grand Prix, an event won by his team-mate Dick Seaman.

ABOVE: Mercedes' Rudolf Caracciola talks to Alfred Neubauer, 1938.

BELOW: Two Auto Union Type D racers head a pair of Mercedes-Benz W154s at the start of the 1938 Donington Grand Prix, with Tazio Nuvolari in the lead.

ENCLOSURE 1: A panoramic photograph of the Nurburgring, taken in 1937.

ENCLOSURE 2: A 1938 sketch of the "Maestro" Tazio Nuvolari by Judy Zeeman.

ENCLOSURES 3 AND 4: Two Mercedes-Benz obituary notices, for Dick Seaman who crashed to his death when leading the 1939 Belgian Grand Prix at Spa-Francorchamps.

The next major change came in 1938, with new limits on weight and engine size (see sidebar). Already, though, Rosemeyer was gone, killed when his Auto Union flipped at 400kph in a speed record attempt. Nuvolari did his best for Auto Union, but Mercedes-Benz had again produced the best car, the W154, and it won the first three races through von Brauchitsch, Dick Seaman – who won the German Grand Prix when a German driver would have been preferred on the top step of the podium – and Caracciola. Then, with development having paid off, Nuvolari won at Monza and Donington Park for Auto Union.

The decade was brought to a close with Auto Union fitting two-stage superchargers to its Type D to reduce its power deficit to Mercedes-Benz. Sadly, the season started with the death of Seaman, trapped in his burning Mercedes-Benz W163 at Spa. The German marques traded wins, with drivers in Alfa Romeos, Delahayes and Talbots picking up the scraps before it all came to a close with the start of the Second World War.

FRANCE
SPIRITUAL HOME OF RACING

The record books show that Grand Prix racing has been dominated by the Italians, the Germans and then the British, but France can truly claim to be its home.

While there can be arguments for and against France being the home of motor racing, it is indisputably the sport's birthplace. Since it held the first grand prix, at Le Mans in 1906, 16 other circuits have hosted the French Grand Prix, among which Reims was famous for its slipstreaming battles, Rouen-les-Essarts for its cobbled hairpin and Clermont-Ferrand for its twists and dippers, and of which the most recent was Magny-Cours, where the race was held until 2008.

The enthusiasm for all forms of motor sport has been strong in France ever since that first road race in 1894, and in the early part of the twentieth century there were numerous companies that went racing to help promote their road cars. Renault was the pace-setter, with Peugeot soon pushing it. They survive as major manufacturers to this day, but the likes of Darracq, Mors and Brasier have long since disappeared.

Cities fought to host the grand prix. Dieppe took over from Le Mans in 1907, Amiens had a go in 1913, then Lyons, Strasbourg and Tours before it went to Montlhéry. The Miramas circuit near Marseilles was next, in 1926, then St Gaudens at Comminges near the Spanish border. The Pau street circuit just to the west in the Pyrenees had its turn in 1930, but there was a breakthrough in 1932 when the French Grand Prix was held by Reims for the first time, with its triangular route of public roads ensuring brilliant racing as it was wide enough for cars to hunt in slipstreaming packs.

ABOVE: The Montlhéry circuit outside Paris provided Louis Chiron (Alfa Romeo P3) with the first of his two solo wins there in 1934.

RIGHT: Reims hosted some of the most exciting French GPs. This is Tony Brooks's winning Ferrari (24) and Jack Brabham's Cooper at the start in 1959.

BELOW: The Rouen-les-Essarts circuit was tricky, but Dan Gurney liked it, giving Brabham its first win in 1964.

ENCLOSURE: The official programme for the 1957 French Grand Prix at Rouen-les-Essarts, an event won for Maserati by Juan Manuel Fangio.

The next circuit given the honour of hosting the French Grand Prix was Rouen-les-Essarts, a difficult, undulating course through a pine forest outside the city. Reims was still the regular home for the race, but Rouen was used on and off until 1968. By then, another circuit had been brought into the rotation. This was at Clermont-Ferrand, an industrial city in the Massif Central, and the twisty circuit was considered by many as France's version of Germany's Nurburgring Nordschleife. The list of winners there only included World Champions.

Le Mans hosted a second grand prix in 1967, on the short Bugatti circuit that uses much of the area behind the paddock for the main circuit.

There was a complete change in 1971 as the French took their grand prix to the purpose-built Paul Ricard circuit at Le Castellet, north-west of Toulon. It was fast, flat and open, and couldn't have been more different from Clermont-Ferrand. Jackie Stewart raced to victory in his Tyrrell 003.

The grand prix moved in 1974 to Dijon-Prenois, a picturesque circuit in Burgundy that had to be lengthened for the three further French Grands Prix it hosted and the one Swiss Grand Prix, held there in 1982 as racing was banned within Switzerland.

In 1991, Paul Ricard was sidelined and the race was moved to Magny-Cours, an upgraded club circuit 150 miles south of Paris. It was an odd

brief period between the late 1970s and the mid-1980s, French cars have been also-rans. The two teams that took them to glory were Ligier and Renault. Ligier won with Jacques Laffite, Patrick Depailler and Didier Pironi between 1977 and 1981 and then a one-off for Olivier Panis in the wet at Monaco in 1996. Renault made its debut in 1977 and started winning in 1979, with 14 more wins added to their tally by Jean-Pierre Jabouille, René Arnoux, Alain Prost and Patrick Tambay up to 1984.

Such has been the French racing industry's decline that even the second-generation Renault team is based in England, with its engines from France. Since government funding for drivers was stopped in the 1990s, the supply of rising stars has all but dried up too. Indeed, Alain Prost has been their only World Champion, a feat he achieved four times, all with British teams.

To make space on the calendar for F1's global expansion, France lost its grand prix after 2008 but is fighting to get it back, although this might take the construction of a new circuit or even alternating with the similarly financially beleaguered Belgian GP.

MONTLHÉRY

Built in 1924, this unusual combination of road circuit and banked oval south-west of Paris hosted the French Grand Prix in 1925. Sadly, its grand prix debut was marked by the death of Antonio Ascari, who flew over the banking, but the circuit soon became the best in France. French marques Delage and Bugatti cleaned up in the first few grands prix, but then Maserati, Alfa Romeo and Mercedes-Benz all tasted success until 1936, when it was decided that the race should be run for sportscars. Yet, after two years of this format, the French Grand Prix was taken to Reims for 1938, and after the Second World War Montlhéry became used chiefly for national events, the most famous being the Paris 1000Kms sportscar race. And so its fortunes declined, and the circuit was closed in 1973. There was a racing revival in 1994, for the FIA GT Championship, but the shortened track was too bumpy and the revival didn't last.

place to go, but government money had paid for the upgrade. Sadly, its location meant crowds weren't huge and, with replacement venues being sought, it declared in 2008 that it couldn't afford to carry on hosting the French Grand Prix, leaving France without a grand prix for the first time since the start of the World Championship, with the exception of 1955 when the French Grand Prix was cancelled following the Le Mans disaster.

France's Formula One involvement goes beyond its all but unbroken run of hosting a grand prix, as the success of Delage, Bugatti and Talbot through the 1920s and 1930s kept it competitive out on the tracks. Indeed, Bugatti in particular gave the French cause for pride as it took the battle to the Italians and, later and less successfully, to the Germans.

Lago-Talbots packed out the grids in the early 1950s, but apart from a

LEFT: Clermont-Ferrand's lap was long and undulating, but Jacky Ickx showed how he was prepared to really attack it in 1969, racing to third for Brabham.

RIGHT: Jean-Pierre Jabouille gave Renault its first F1 win in an exciting finish in 1979 at Dijon-Prenois.

BELOW: Damon Hill chases his Williams team-mate Alain Prost into Magny-Cours' Adelaide hairpin in 1993, when Prost won by a fraction of a second.

THE 1940s
WARTIME AND AUSTERITY

It's no surprise that there was little racing in Europe in the 1940s, but the will was there to pick up the pieces after the Second World War, even if the cars were a little old.

The privations of wartime meant that motor racing took a back seat, with manufacturing capacity being focused on munitions rather than motor cars. When the Second World War ended and petrol rationing gradually eased, grand prix racing grew and grew, soon taking place almost weekly from early spring to late autumn.

The first post-war race meeting was held on 9 September 1945 on a road circuit laid out around the Bois de Boulogne just outside Paris. Three races were held, and the first for small sportscars was the Robert Benoist Trophy, in memory of the former Delage and Bugatti driver who had been shot by the Gestapo. Victory went to Amédée Gordini, who would go on to build grand prix cars. The main race, the Coupe des Prisonniers, was won by 1936 French Grand Prix winner Jean-Pierre Wimille in a Bugatti.

So, racing was under way again and people were already hatching great plans for the future, developing the ideas and machinery that would put them at the sharp end of the field at the start of the 1950s. Among the various meetings of minds, Enzo Ferrari contacted Alfa Romeo designer Gioacchino Colombo and they hatched plans for an engine that would become Ferrari's mainstay: the V12.

What was notable in 1946 was how many street circuits were used, at Nice, Marseilles, Geneva, Milan, Turin and Paris, as the desire to go racing again outstripped the number of permanent circuits, although these soon started to be rebuilt or begun from scratch. Among these new circuits was Silverstone, on a layout around a Second World War airfield in Northamptonshire, England, which would be open for business in 1948.

Through 1946, though, the dusted-down Alfa Romeo 158s were soon cleaning up on every appearance, but they were poorly prepared for their first race back, at St Cloud, and victory went to Raymond Sommer in a Maserati. Thereafter, it was all Alfa Romeo.

Until 1947, the assorted races were all minor events, and only in 1947 did a series of international races begin, when cars ran to what would become Formula One regulations for the first time, with 4500cc normally-aspirated or 1500cc supercharged engines. This increased the ratio between normally-aspirated and supercharged cars, but it suited Alfa Romeo's 1500cc supercharged 158s which pushed out the most power, 275bhp, and the Italian steamroller carried on. Wimille and Count Carlo-Felice Trossi were victorious at Bremgarten, near Berne, at Spa-Francorchamps and on the Milan street circuit that stood in while the Monza circuit was tidied up after its wartime use as something of a dumping ground. The Italian marque skipped the French Grand Prix, though, and Louis Chiron won at Lyons in a Lago-Talbot single-seater. This French-built car, based on a sportscar, was nothing like as quick as the Alfa Romeos or as powerful as the Maseratis, but it was economical and reliable and so picked up numerous placings in the minor races, which was important as prize money was what kept most racers going in those days.

The Alfa 158s also stayed away from the first international grand prix of 1948 at Monaco, where Giuseppe Farina won for Maserati. There was one win for Trossi in Switzerland, where team-mate Achille Varzi was killed in practice when his 158 inverted after a series of spins. Proving how dangerous racing was in the days before roll hoops and thus before seat harnesses, the race itself claimed the life of Christian Kautz, who crashed his Maserati. Trossi's win was followed by two for Wimille, at Reims and in the wet on the Valentino Park street circuit in Turin. Then Alfa Romeo elected not to travel to the inaugural British Grand Prix at Silverstone, but Italian pride

LEFT: Giuseppe Farina gives Ferrari its first grand prix appearance in the 1948 Italian GP in Turin. The race was held on a circuit in Turin's Valentino Park as Monza was undergoing repairs.

BELOW: Alfa Romeo 158s lead the way as Achille Varzi heads eventual race winner Jean-Pierre Wimille at the downhill start of the 1947 Belgian Grand Prix at Spa-Francorchamps.

was kept intact with Luigi Villoresi leading Alberto Ascari in a Maserati one-two ahead of Bob Gerard in a sit-up-and-beg ERA, the pre-war British racer that was the staple on the British racing scene until the 1950s.

Making it easier for their rivals, Alfa Romeo sat out 1949, smarting from the loss of Varzi midway through 1948, then Wimille in Argentina and Trossi to a lengthy illness, and it was left to Baron Emanuel de Graffenried to set the season rolling by winning the British Grand Prix for Maserati. Louis Rosier gave the Lago-Talbot 26C its first major win, in the Belgian Grand Prix, with Chiron adding a second at the French Grand Prix, but then a new marque started winning – and it's still winning today. This was Ferrari, whose first purpose-built grand prix car, the 125, had made its debut towards the end of the 1948 season and was a winner by mid-1949, with Ascari winning the Swiss Grand Prix at Bremgarten and later in the year the Italian Grand Prix. British racer Peter Whitehead rounded out 1949 by winning the Czech Grand Prix on the fearsome Brno road circuit.

And so the racing scene had got back on to an even keel and, with manufacturers anxious to boost their names with success on the racing scene, it was time for something bigger and better organized, the Formula One World Championship which would start with the new decade.

ABOVE: Alberto Ascari powers away from team-mate Luigi Villoresi at the start of the 1949 Italian GP on his way to victory for Ferrari.

RIGHT: Luigi Villoresi's Ferrari (20), Juan Manuel Fangio's Maserati (34) and Louis Rosier's Talbot line up on the front row for the 1949 French GP.

BELOW: This Auto Union Awtowelo 650 from the late 1940s shows how car design might have proceeded had the Second World War not got in the way.

BELOW: Luigi Villoresi wears the traditional victor's garland after winning the 1948 British GP at Silverstone for Maserati ahead of his team-mate Alberto Ascari.

ENCLOSURE: A letter from Field-Marshal Montgomery explaining why he didn't feel in 1948 that Donington Park was suitable to revert to being a racing venue.

THE 1950s
BRAVE NEW WORLD

The World Championship was launched in 1950, but the teams at the top had to fight to stay there and the rear-engined revolution was set to change everything.

From 1950, there would be a series of races for Formula One cars to decide an overall World Champion. The first race took place at Silverstone and it was the start of something great.

There were 21 cars, but Alfa Romeo's Giuseppe Farina, Luigi Fagioli, Juan Manuel Fangio and Reg Parnell filled the first four grid slots before Farina won from Fagioli and Parnell after Fangio retired. Yves Giraud-Cabantous was best of the rest, two laps down in his Lago-Talbot.

The remainder of 1950 was all Alfa Romeo, although Ferrari turned up for the next race, in Monaco, and did well, with Alberto Ascari following Fangio home in second. The race was a lottery, though, as an accident on lap one claimed nine cars, including two of the Alfa Romeos.

Normal service resumed at the Swiss Grand Prix and Farina and Fagioli gave Alfa a one-two after Fangio retired. Again a Lago-Talbot, Louis Rosier's, was the best of the rest after both Ferraris showed speed then retired. Alfa Romeo won the remaining three races, and Farina was crowned World Champion.

In 1951, Alfa Romeo were challenged by Ferrari, who scored their breakthrough win, with José Froilan Gonzalez leading home Fangio in the British Grand Prix after Fangio had to bring his 159 in for an extra fuel stop and stalled. Inspired by this, Ascari won for Ferrari at the German Grand Prix, and again at Monza, although Fangio would go on to be crowned champion after winning the final race.

The rules were changed for 1952 in an attempt to lure more manufacturers to enter cars, and Alfa Romeo chose to withdraw rather than run cars to Formula Two rules, which meant 2000cc or 500cc supercharged engines. This suited Ferrari and it attracted cars from Cooper, Connaught, Frazer Nash, Gordini and HWM as a host of racing car manufacturers made their first steps towards what would, for some, be glory. Ascari missed the opening race as he was qualifying for the

RIGHT: A Dunlop Racing tyre mounted on a wobbly web wheel.

ABOVE: Alberto Ascari started from pole position and led every lap to win the 1952 French GP at Rouen-les-Essarts for Ferrari.

TOP: This rudimentary crash helmet belonging to Jose Froilan Gonzalez has holes cut in it for ventilation.

BELOW RIGHT: Ferrari's Jose Froilan Gonzalez attempts to keep Juan Manuel Fangio's Mercedes behind him in the 1954 German GP, but the Argentinian was soon in front, going on to win.

GIUSEPPE FARINA

When Giuseppe "Nino" Farina started racing, he was taught by the great Tazio Nuvolari. He won the Italian drivers' title in 1937, 1938 and 1939 and was in a strong position to land a top drive when the Second World War ended. Although he quit the Alfa Romeo team in 1946, "Nino" returned for 1950 and won the first World Championship title by winning three of the year's six races (below). He couldn't match team-mate Juan Manuel Fangio in 1951 and ended up fourth overall, having won only the Belgian Grand Prix. Then he joined Ferrari for 1952, but he won only non-championship races until he took the 1953 German Grand Prix after team leader Alberto Ascari lost a wheel. "Nino" suffered burns in a sportscar race in 1954 and didn't race again until 1955. However, this return wasn't to last long as the pain from his injuries forced him to dose himself with morphine and he elected to retire.

Indy 500, with victory going to his Ferrari team-mate Piero Taruffi, but he won the remaining six races to land the title and carried on winning into 1953, taking the first three before British hotshot Mike Hawthorn came out on top of a scrap with Fangio to win the French Grand Prix for Ferrari. Only Maserati, through Fangio, stopped a second Ferrari whitewash by winning the final round when leader Ascari spun on the final lap.

New 2500cc Formula One rules were introduced for 1954 and this coaxed Mercedes-Benz back. And how! They didn't arrive until Fangio had given the Maserati 250F a couple of wins, but the German team's desire to win was evident on its debut at the French Grand Prix when it clad its W196s with wheel-enclosing bodywork and raced to a one-two, with Fangio having changed teams to keep on winning. These bodies didn't work at Silverstone, and Gonzalez led home Hawthorn in a Ferrari one-two, but the Germans won three on the trot before Hawthorn rounded out the year with victory in Spain, in a race in which Lancia made its debut and Ascari started from pole and led the race but retired.

The 1955 season was all Mercedes save for Monaco, when both Fangio and rising British star Stirling Moss retired, and Ascari flipped his Ferrari into the harbour, leaving Maurice Trintignant to win for Ferrari. Ascari was uninjured but crashed a sportscar a few days later and died.

Moss had finished the Belgian and Dutch Grands Prix on Fangio's tail, but the understudy's day would come, at the British Grand Prix at Aintree, when Fangio led but was overtaken – perhaps allowed himself to be. The great Argentinian never let on.

One event a month earlier led to Switzerland banning racing and to Mercedes-Benz quitting at the end of the year. This was an accident in the Le Mans 24 Hours when a car flew into the crowd, killing nearly 100 people.

Mercedes-Benz's withdrawal left the way clear for Ferrari in 1956. Its parent company, Fiat, had taken over Lancia, so Fangio was equipped with the car that started life as the Lancia D50. Fangio raced to his fourth title, but clinched it only with the help of team-mate Peter Collins who, on realizing that Fangio's car was damaged in the finale, handed over his own. Had he not, he could have been champion...

Moss had pushed Fangio hard in 1956 and swapped his Maserati for a Vanwall for 1957. He was anxious to win in a British car, which he did, but Fangio won more in a Maserati and was champion for a fifth time. His most notable drive was in the German Grand Prix when a fuel stop left him 45 seconds behind the Ferraris, which he chased, caught and passed.

Vanwall's challenge grew in 1958 and Tony Brooks bagged three wins. Going into the final round, Hawthorn, with just one win, had the most points. Moss had to win and did, but Brooks's engine blew and Phil Hill ushered Hawthorn through to the title. Perhaps most notable was that Moss had opened the season, in Argentina, winning in a rear-engined Cooper. This was the start of the end for front-engined cars.

The 1959 season was one of flux. Vanwall withdrew following the death of Stuart Lewis-Evans from injuries from the last race of 1958; BRM finally scored its first win, but Cooper came good and sounded the death knell for front-engined cars as Jack Brabham took the battle to the Ferraris and came out on top.

LEFT: Stirling Moss struck a blow for progress in Argentina in 1958 when he took this Cooper to the first victory by a car with its engine behind the driver.

ABOVE: Harry Schell drives his Vanwall past Tony Brooks's burning BRM out of Abbey Corner at the 1956 British GP. Brooks survived, but the car didn't...

BELOW: Vanwall introduced true streamlining to Formula One and this example from 1957 sports the then traditional British racing green livery.

ENCLOSURE 1: Letter and a telegram sent and received by Tazio Nuvolari in 1951. Upon his return to racing after the War, he was 54 and suffering from ill-health.

ENCLOSURE 2: A letter about Argentinian great Juan Manuel Fangio from 1954.

ENCLOSURE 3: A poster for the non-championship 1957 Australian GP at Caversham.

SILVERSTONE
WHERE IT ALL BEGAN

Fast, open and constantly changing shape, that's Silverstone, but it's more than that as it has hosted some stunning races and is still a challenge to drive.

A disused RAF airfield in the Midlands was an unassuming place to see the start of a global competition, but Silverstone hosted the first ever World Championship grand prix. It remains, at least until 2009, one of the toughest but fairest tests for drivers, with a selection of fast corners, esses and a long straight. Thereafter, however, its future as the home of the British Grand Prix is uncertain, as Bernie Ecclestone has tired of years of negotiation with Silverstone's owners, the British Racing Drivers Club, about the changes he wants to the circuit and its facilities. From 2010 onwards, the race will be held at Donington Park providing that the circuit undergoes considerable modification.

Silverstone hosted the British Grand Prix for the first time in 1948, but it was the third running of the event in 1950 that is most frequently but erroneously recalled as the first event, as this was when the World Championship burst into life. Luigi Villoresi won in 1948 for Maserati, and the circuit's wide-open nature was markedly different from the Bremgarten circuit that hosted that year's Swiss Grand Prix and the Turin circuit that was the temporary home of the Italian Grand Prix. Maserati won again, through Emanuel de Graffenried, in 1949.

Attracting huge crowds, the British Grand Prix went from strength to strength through the 1950s, with a change of venue coming in 1955 when the Aintree circuit near Liverpool, running in front of the grandstands used for the Grand National horse race, started an alternation programme with Silverstone that lasted until 1963. After that, the undulating Brands Hatch circuit took over as Silverstone's alternating partner and this relationship ran until 1986, since when Silverstone has had sole hosting rights, until Donington Park snatched the race for 2010.

Stirling Moss's maiden win at Aintree in 1955 stands out as one of the famous British Grands Prix, when he moved ahead of Mercedes team-mate Juan Manuel Fangio. Two years later, he won at Aintree again, sharing his Vanwall with Tony Brooks, and this marked the first World Championship win for a British car.

From 1962 to 1967, it didn't appear to matter where the race was held, as Jim Clark would win it, taking five wins from six.

The next theme that settled on the British Grand Prix was one of havoc. Jody Scheckter set the ball rolling in 1973 when he ran wide in his McLaren out of Woodcote at the end of the opening lap and scattered the following cars like skittles, leaving eight cars on the sidelines. The 1974 race at Brands Hatch had a ridiculous conclusion as race leader Niki Lauda had to make a late pitstop to replace a disintegrating tyre and found the pit exit blocked by an official's car and a crowd of hangers-on. Then the 1975 race was hit by a cloudburst at the far end of the circuit, leaving 12 cars in the catch-fencing at Stowe and Club. Emerson Fittipaldi, who had made it past the scene while those chasing him slid off, called at the pits and was changing to rain tyres when it was adjudged too hazardous to continue and he was declared the winner.

Any hopes that 1976 would be trouble-free were expelled when James Hunt's McLaren was tipped skywards at the first corner by Clay Regazzoni, who was pitched into a spin by

SILVERSTONE CIRCUIT

Silverstone was born out of the desire to go racing after the Second World War and the need to do something with a wartime airfield. The one constant has been that its nature offers fast, open racing, but its layout has changed considerably. When it opened in 1948, the start line was just after Abbey, with Woodcote as the first corner. It made use of the runways and was shaped like an anvil when it held the first British Grand Prix that year. The circuit gained its traditional outline in 1949 when it moved to a layout using more perimeter roads, with long straights and fast corners. It became known as a circuit with a good flow that afforded plenty of overtaking opportunities. The start was moved to between Woodcote and Copse in 1950; chicanes have been added and esses inserted after Maggotts; Stowe has been tightened and the whole Brooklands complex added, but the nature of the Silverstone circuit stays the same.

trying to pass Ferrari team-mate Lauda into Paddock Hill Bend. The race was stopped and the controversy came from Hunt diving into the back entrance of the pits. He was told that he wouldn't be allowed to take the restart, but the crowd went wild and the decision was reversed. Hunt went on to win but was later disqualified.

Fortunately, the race calmed down from 1977, with Regazzoni taking a popular first win for Williams at Silverstone in 1979.

Nigel Mansell rounded out Brands Hatch's run of hosting the race in 1986 with a win, but his most famous British Grand Prix victories as he became the darling of the home crowd came on the flat-out blasts around Silverstone. His charge to victory at Silverstone in 1987, from 28 seconds down on his Williams team-mate Nelson Piquet after a pitstop, will never be forgotten. His classic manoeuvre to take the lead with just three laps remaining, feinting one way then diving the other into Stowe, sent the crowd into a frenzy.

Double World Champion Graham Hill never won the British Grand Prix, but his son Damon did, in 1994, and fellow British racers Johnny Herbert and David Coulthard also put their names on the victory roll. However, perhaps the most infamous race as the twentieth century came to a close was the 1998 British Grand Prix when Michael Schumacher won the race while entering the pits for a stop-go penalty for passing a rival under a yellow (hazard) flag. It was controversial and typical of a race that seldom fails to excite.

Hamiltonmania added thousands to the gate, including many first-time race visitors in 2007, but the greatest change came in 2010 when the run from Abbey to Brooklands via Bridge was replaced with a new infield loop and inner straight. In 2011, this was augmented by a new pit building and the moving of the startline to between Club and Abbey.

ENCLOSURE 1: Pages and the lap chart for the second British Grand Prix that was held at Silverstone in 1949, showing how Emanuel de Graffenried advanced to victory for Maserati.

ENCLOSURE 2: Seven years later and now a round of the world championship, this lap chart for the 1956 British Grand Prix show how gearbox failure cost Stirling Moss victory and let Juan Manuel Fangio through to win.

BELOW: Silverstone's new pits, hospitality and media building, known as The Wing, dwarfs the new start/finish straight, with the track now turning right at Abbey.

JUAN MANUEL FANGIO
THE GRAND MASTER

There was nothing this Argentinian ace couldn't do in a car, and Juan Manuel's five world titles in the 1950s were proof of this as he changed teams to keep his advantage.

Although Giuseppe Farina won the inaugural World Championship, the first Formula One legend was Argentinian racer Juan Manuel Fangio, who was World Champion five times in the 1950s. Across the first eight years of Formula One, he drove in only 51 grands prix yet won 24. Arguably the finest driver ever, he never seemed out of control and was so versatile that he was World Champion for four manufacturers: Alfa Romeo, Mercedes-Benz, Maserati and Ferrari. What is more, in contrast to today's child kartists who hit Formula One by their very early twenties, Juan Manuel was 37 when he first raced a single-seater and 46 when he claimed his fifth and final title.

The son of an Italian immigrant, Juan Manuel was born in Balcarce and had his first racing experience riding as a mechanic in a Chevrolet driven by a customer of the garage where he worked. He then took the wheel himself and raced in hazardous road races with much success, winning the 1940 Gran Premio del Nacional in a works Chevrolet.

Racing returned in 1947 and Juan Manuel was fascinated by visiting Italians Achille Varzi and Luigi Villoresi, especially as the Argentine Automobile Club had bought two Maseratis to be driven against them and he was entrusted with one of them. Inspired by the experience, Juan Manuel went racing in Europe, but he came close to quitting when, on a return trip home, he crashed in a road race and killed his co-driver.

At the start of 1949, with the backing of President Perón, he won the Mar del Plata Grand Prix, and went back to Europe carrying the hopes of a nation. He started winning, most notably at the Monza Grand Prix,

when he beat the works Ferraris with one purchased by the ACA.

As Alfa Romeo prepared for the first World Championship in 1950, Juan Manuel was given a drive. He won three grands prix, at Monaco, Spa-Francorchamps and Reims, but was pipped by team-mate Farina. However, staying with Alfa Romeo, he gained the first of his five world titles the following season after winning the Swiss, French and Spanish Grands Prix to outscore Ferrari's Alberto Ascari.

The Alfa Romeo 159 was now past its sell-by date, and Alfa Romeo decided to quit the sport rather than invest more to build a new car to suit the incoming Formula Two regulations that were to be adopted for 1952, so Juan Manuel moved to Maserati. However, after winning six non-championship races in Argentina, Juan Manuel broke his neck in an accident at Monza, which kept him off the track until 1953.

This might have slowed a lesser driver, but when Juan Manuel returned with Maserati, he was able to finish as runner-up to Ferrari's Ascari despite not winning until the final round at Monza when he came out best from a four-way final corner incident. He also won the Carrera Panamericana road race across Mexico.

Then came Juan Manuel's incredible run of four straight world titles. He won the first couple of races in 1954 in a Maserati, but when Mercedes-Benz's new car was ready he switched teams and then won another four races that year before waltzing to a third straight title in 1955, picking up four wins as he provided a masterclass to team-mate Stirling Moss.

Because of a disaster during the Le Mans 24 Hours in which nearly 100 people were killed when a car flew into the crowd,

Mercedes-Benz quit at the end of the year, and so Juan Manuel moved on to Ferrari. After he won the Argentinian, British and French Grands Prix, the championship became a battle between Fangio, his team-mate Peter Collins and Maserati's Moss. At the final round at Monza, the steering on Juan Manuel's Ferrari failed but Collins thought nothing of handing over his own car to help his team leader win the title.

Having not enjoyed the management style at Ferrari, Juan Manuel rejoined Maserati for 1957 and won the championship for the last time. The race that clinched it was his greatest: the German Grand Prix at the Nurburgring (see sidebar). Although older than his rivals, he had enormous staying power, Vanwall's Moss being the only driver capable of giving him a hard time, but his run of four wins in the first five races showed that he was still the gold standard.

In 1958, Juan Manuel finished fourth in his home grand prix, then missed three races before making his final World Championship outing in the French Grand Prix, also finishing fourth. Between these two events, though, he had been in the newspapers for a different reason: while in Havana to contest the Cuban sportscar grand prix, he was kidnapped. Juan Manuel missed the race but was then released unharmed, his captors pleased to have had the oxygen of publicity for Fidel Castro's coming revolution.

Juan Manuel's retirement was spent running a chain of Mercedes dealerships in Argentina and being a roving ambassador up until his death in 1995.

BELOW: Fangio keeps his Lancia-Ferrari D50 ahead of Stirling Moss's Maserati 250F in the 1956 Argentinian GP, on his way to starting his campaign with a win.

RIGHT: Juan Manuel Fangio lines up with fellow world champions at the 1990 Australian GP in Adelaide. Back row, left to right: James Hunt, Jackie Stewart, Denny Hulme. Front row: Nelson Piquet, Fangio, Ayrton Senna and Jack Brabham.

THE GREATEST RACE

The 1957 German Grand Prix wasn't only Fangio's greatest ever race: it was possibly the greatest race of all, and the greatest comeback, on the toughest circuit of all. He qualified his Maserati 250F on pole, slashing 16 seconds off the lap record around this 14-mile circuit, but was led around the first two laps by Ferrari's Mike Hawthorn and Peter Collins. On lap three, he passed them and hared away, knowing that he would have to stop for fuel and rear tyres, and they would not. Before pitting at mid-distance, he was 28 seconds clear, and rejoined 30 seconds behind. Collins was now flying. There were 11 laps left, and Fangio said that he drove each lap like a qualifier and he reeled them in, catching them by 6 seconds each lap. Two laps from home, he lapped 8 seconds faster than his pole lap and caught the Ferraris with a lap and a half to go. They couldn't resist him. Not bad for a 46-year-old...

SIR STIRLING MOSS
THE BEST WORLD CHAMPION WE NEVER HAD

He was a pupil of Juan Manuel Fangio's and beat him from time to time but somehow never managed to pick up a world title despite being easily good enough to do so.

LEFT: Stirling Moss made his World Championship debut in this little HWM in the 1951 Swiss GP, finishing eighth.

It's universally accepted that Sir Stirling Moss, as he now is, remains the finest driver never to win a World Championship. His Formula One career lasted from 1951 to 1961 before being brought to an end by a terrible crash at Goodwood at the start of 1962, but his record of 16 wins in 66 races is one of the best hit rates ever. For four consecutive years, 1955–58, he finished runner-up in the Drivers' World Championship, but he deserves even more praise for his incredible ability to hop into any type of car and be a winner in it.

From a family steeped in racing, with both parents having raced, Stirling was always likely to follow suit and soon moved from a BMW 328 sportscar in 1947 into single-seaters, racing a Cooper Formula Three car with considerable success. But, as would be the case throughout his career, he raced sportscars too, winning the Tourist Trophy in a Jaguar XK120 in 1950. His World Championship debut followed in 1951 at the then unusually early age of 21. This was in an

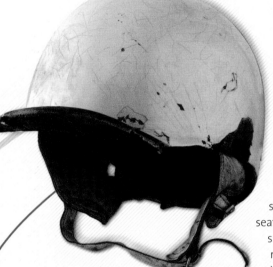

ABOVE: This white cork helmet was Stirling Moss's trademark throughout his career. He continued to wear it until he stopped racing in June 2011.

HWM, but there was no likelihood of success against the might of the Alfa Romeos and Ferraris. This was the story of the next few years as Moss raced an HWM again, an ERA, a Connaught and then a Cooper. All were British marques, Stirling being fiercely patriotic, but it became clear that he was going to have to drive a continental-built chassis if he wanted to place higher than his best result to this point: sixth place in the 1953 German Grand Prix.

Ferrari had been interested in his services for 1954, and Moss was hoping to attract Mercedes-Benz, but neither move came off, so his family team bought a Maserati 250F and Stirling bagged a third place on their World Championship debut in the Belgian Grand Prix. Then, when Juan Manuel Fangio transferred to the Mercedes team mid-season, Stirling joined the works Maserati effort.

ABOVE: Moss crosses the finishing line at Aintree in 1955 for his first World Championship win. Mercedes team-mate Juan Manuel Fangio follows in his wake.

BELOW LEFT: Vanwall chief Tony Vandervell (holding trophy) celebrates with Tony Brooks and Moss (right) after their shared win in the 1957 British GP.

Although he failed to record a finish with the Maserati team, his obvious speed had been noticed by Mercedes-Benz competition boss Alfred Neubauer, most notably when he led the Italian Grand Prix. As a result, Stirling was a Mercedes driver for 1955, and he shadowed Fangio until the British Grand Prix, when he passed the great man to score his first grand prix win. It was never clear whether his mentor had let him by.

Mercedes withdrawal at the end of 1955 left Stirling out of a ride, and Maserati snapped him up as its number one. He won at Monaco and Monza, but poor mechanical reliability left him second to Fangio.

Vanwall gave Moss his first ride in a competitive British Formula One car in 1957, and Stirling finished the year as runner-up behind Fangio for the third year in succession. Nevertheless he was very much the class act in the second half of the season, adding victories in the Pescara and Italian Grands Prix to his earlier success at Aintree when he took over from Tony Brooks mid-race after his team-mate, still suffering from leg injuries, began to tire.

Vanwall became stronger still in 1958, these most streamlined of cars winning six of the 10 races, but Stirling had already got his season rolling at the Argentinian Grand Prix, which Vanwall skipped. He drove a blinder in searing heat to win in Rob Walker's Cooper, thus taking the

LEFT: John Surtees was world champion for Ferrari in 1964, but after quitting two races into 1966 he was a winner for Cooper in Mexico. Jack Brabham gives chase.

RIGHT: Jim Clark and Lotus principal Colin Chapman remain one of Formula One's greatest partnerships.

BELOW: Jackie Stewart won at Silverstone for Matra in 1969, then went on to win the first of his three world titles.

BOTTOM: The cigar-shaped Lotus 25, powered by a Climax engine, was the class of 1963 in Jim Clark's hands.

The engine rules were changed for 1966, with a 3-litre formula being introduced. It looked as though Ferrari was again best prepared. Stewart had won the opening race with a 2-litre engine in his BRM, but that was at Monaco. Ferrari won the next race, at Spa-Francorchamps, but Surtees quit the team and it lost momentum. Then Jack Brabham scored consecutive wins at Reims, Brands Hatch, Zandvoort and the Nurburgring, powered by an Australian-sourced Repco V8, to claim his third title. The start of that run, the French Grand Prix, was the first grand prix win for a driver in a car bearing his own name.

The most notable event of the decade came in 1967, and it would have ramifications until the 1980s. This was the introduction of the Cosworth DFV, a V8 engine financed by Ford that would lead to the arrival of numerous teams using its off-the-shelf V8s to make their mark. The DFV debuted at Zandvoort where Clark gave it a winning start. He would win three more times that year, but the title went to Brabham's Denny Hulme.

ENCLOSURE 1: Cutaway drawings were exceptionally popular in the 1960s. This is a Brian Hatton drawing of BRM's P57, with which Graham Hill won the 1962 title.

ENCLOSURE 2: A cutaway of the 1969 four-wheel-drive Lotus-DFV 63 by Dick Ellis.

Clark also won the 1968 opener, but the world of motor racing was then shocked when the popular Scot was killed in a Formula Two race. Lotus supremacy was challenged, but Graham Hill kept the team positive and won the title. The year was also notable for the start of a trend that continues today: the use of aerodynamic wings. Nose tabs were followed by low rear wings, then high-mounted aerofoils.

Concerns about the strut-mounted wings were justified at the 1969 Spanish Grand Prix, when both Lotuses had their wings collapse, pitching them into barriers. Wings were much reduced after that, and the team that handled this best was Matra, run by Ken Tyrrell, with Stewart winning six times to become the fourth British World Champion in a thoroughly British decade.

SPA-FRANCORCHAMPS
TAKING THE FOREST PATH

This Belgian circuit is surely the template for the perfect circuit, with gradient changes, challenging corners, beautiful scenery and the ever-present possibility of rain to mix it up.

ABOVE: Juan Manuel Fangio trickles his Alfa Romeo down from La Source to meet the reception committee after winning the 1950 Belgian GP ahead of Luigi Fagoli.

Set in the Ardennes Forest, Spa-Francorchamps, home of the Belgian Grand Prix on and off since 1925, is the favourite track of almost every racing driver who has ever raced there. It is a very testing circuit, offering spectacular views for spectators, and for proof that quality will out there one only has to look at its list of winners: since 1985, David Coulthard is the only Belgian Grand Prix winner not to win the World Championship in his career.

This great event was held for the first time in 1925, when it was won by Antonio Ascari, the father of Alberto Ascari, World Champion of 1952 and '53. Antonio's Alfa Romeo P2 was quickest around the 9.2-mile circuit from Francorchamps to Malmedy to Stavelot and back that started in one valley, rose over a hill and dropped into a second valley before making the return journey through a forest.

Situated high in the Ardennes Forest, the Spa-Francorchamps circuit was famous for being hit by rain, and often only locally. One end of the circuit would be drenched while the other end would remain bone dry, making it treacherous indeed.

Jim Clark, who became the king of the circuit from 1962 to 1965, professed to loathe the place, heaving a sigh of relief every time that he left there alive, no doubt as a direct result of the deaths and injuries that he witnessed on his first visit there in 1960 (see sidebar).

In 1972 the Belgian Grand Prix was moved to Nivelles. This was

partly because average lap speeds were nudging 150mph when Pedro Rodriguez won for BRM in 1970, and increasingly safety-minded drivers considered it too dangerous. These included leading safety campaigner Jackie Stewart, who had crashed in a rainstorm in 1966 and ended up trapped in his inverted BRM, soaked in petrol but unable to remove the steering wheel. He always raced with a spanner fixed in the cockpit after that. The other reason had to do with Belgian politics: it was thought desirable for the Flemish-speaking end of the country to have a chance to host the race.

Nivelles, near Brussels, was never popular as it was considered bland in comparison to Spa-Francorchamps, and the race moved on to Zolder, located north-west of Liège, in 1973. Slow and scratchy, with a shortage of high-speed corners, Zolder was also dull and unchallenging in comparison, and the death of Gilles Villeneuve in qualifying there in 1982 started the end of its reign.

By 1983, Spa-Francorchamps was back in the

LEFT: Pedro Rodriguez averaged just under 150mph in his BRM in 1970, in the final grand prix before F1 quit the ultra-fast but unsafe original circuit.

THE DEADLY 1960 BELGIAN GRAND PRIX

Death and injury were sadly all too commonplace in the 1950s and 1960s, but what happened at the Belgian Grand Prix in 1960 was shocking even by the standards of the day. The toll at the end of the race meeting was two drivers dead and two badly injured. All were British, three were driving Lotus cars. Stirling Moss and Mike Taylor both suffered mechanical failure during practice, with Taylor suffering multiple injuries and later suing Lotus for damages after his steering column failed, and Moss crashing after his Lotus lost a wheel at 140mph. Moss wrote in his diary: "Shunt, back, legs, nose, bruises, bugger." Worse was to follow in the race when Chris Bristow lost control of his Cooper when battling with Willy Mairesse and was killed against trackside fencing. Five laps later, Alan Stacey also died after the unluckiest accident of all. Hit in the face by a bird, he collided with a bank and was thrown from his car.

there in 2001 after clashing with Eddie Irvine's Jaguar.

Spa-Francorchamps has produced some epic races, and perhaps the most spectacular of all was in 1998 when there was trouble from start to finish. The first incident wasn't long in coming, with David Coulthard's McLaren being put into a spin on the wet track as he tried to power out of the first corner, the La Source hairpin. The cars then became like balls on a pinball table, crashing into each other. Eight drivers failed to take the restart and Damon Hill led the way in his Jordan until Michael Schumacher pushed his Ferrari to the front and pulled away as the rain intensified. Mid-race, he caught Coulthard who had been delayed and, blinded by the McLaren's spray, ploughed into the back of him, later seeking him out in the pit garages in adversarial mood. This left Hill to give Jordan its first win, with team-mate Ralf Schumacher having to be told not to try to challenge him in case they clashed and the team came away with nothing.

frame, its lap reduced to 4.3 miles in length and confined to just one valley by turning right at the top of the hill, at the corner now called Les Combes, then cutting down the valley side before rejoining the old track at Stavelot corner before Blanchimont on the long climb back to Francorchamps. And here the Belgian Grand Prix has stayed ever since, apart from a few years when money wrangles have led to it being dropped from the World Championship calendar.

Spa-Francorchamps is loved by fans for the spectacle that it offers as it winds its way up and down its terrain through the forest, and also by the drivers for the challenge that it offers. The dipping and bucking Eau Rouge section is considered the toughest of all, and there have been some major accidents here over the years. Alessandro Zanardi, Jacques Villleneuve and Ricardo Zonta all escaped big ones, but Stefan Bellof was killed there, crashing in a sportscar race in 1985. Faster still is Blanchimont, on the climb back towards the pits, and Luciano Burti was unbelievably fortunate to escape with his life when he crashed his Prost

LEFT: Getting Eau Rouge just right has long been tricky, and this is BAR's Ricardo Zonta getting it wrong in 1999, arriving backwards into Raidillon.

RIGHT: Spectators at the top of the track are afforded a brilliant view as the track plunges towards Pouhon. The pits area is in the far background.

BELOW: This is the view back from Raidillon, looking down the descent to the preceding corner, Eau Rouge.

JACK BRABHAM
THE CONSUMMATE ALL-ROUNDER

LEFT: Jack Brabham raced to wins at Monaco and Aintree in his Cooper T51 in 1959 to clinch the first of his three drivers' titles.

BOTTOM LEFT: Jack Brabham and Denny Hulme lead out of the first corner at the 1966 British GP at Brands Hatch, heading towards a one-two, with all rivals lapped.

They don't make drivers like Jack Brabham any more, drivers who have the skill to win grands prix as well as the sheer drive to set up their own teams and win titles.

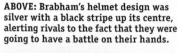

J
ack Brabham became the first Australian to win the Drivers' World Championship when he took the 1959 crown. Seven years later, he became the first driver to be World Champion in a car of his own. As a driver, Jack won three world titles; as a team owner, he won two, with Denny Hulme of New Zealand behind the wheel for the second. The Brabham team raced for 30 years, although Jack ceded interest to his partner Ron Tauranac in 1971.

Like so many antipodean racers who were brought up to "make do and mend", parts not being readily available when he started racing, Jack was someone who got things done. Often incredibly focused, he was known as "Black Jack" – not for an affinity with the gaming tables, but for the colour of his mood when things went wrong or people got in his way.

After a spell maintaining fighter planes for the Australian Air Force, Jack became New South Wales champion in 1948, aged 22, in his first season of racing, in American-style midgets. He then forged an alliance with engineer Tauranac, with whom he would later form Brabham. After becoming Australian hillclimb champion in 1953, the authorities objected to sponsorship on his Cooper, so Brabham went overseas and shone in the 1954 New Zealand Grand Prix.

Feeling that there was far more racing to be had in Europe, Jack headed north in 1955 and became associated with John Cooper, making

his World Championship debut in that year's British Grand Prix, before returning home to win the non-championship Australian GP. Back in Britain for the following year's race, in a privately entered Maserati, Jack was only making up the numbers. However, a part-programme with Cooper in 1957 was far better, although he missed out on third place at Monaco when his fuel pump failed. Jack had done enough to be invited back for a full campaign with Cooper in 1958. He started that year by winning the non-championship New Zealand Grand Prix, then peaked with fourth at Monaco.

By 1959, the tide was running the way of these little rear-engined British racing cars. With 2.5-litre Climax engines, the Cooper was a force, driven by Jack, Stirling Moss, Maurice Trintignant, Bruce McLaren and Masten Gregory. Although Moss took pole for the season opener at Monaco, his car failed and Jack won. He may not have been the quickest, but Jack was consistent. Then, after a pair of podium finishes, he won again at Aintree and sealed his first world title at Sebring despite running out of fuel and having to push his car to the finish in fourth place.

Jack recovered from a slow start to 1960 to win races at Zandvoort, Spa-Francorchamps, Reims, Silverstone and Oporto, to win his second title.

ABOVE: Brabham's helmet design was silver with a black stripe up its centre, alerting rivals to the fact that they were going to have a battle on their hands.

RIGHT: Brabham may be smiling for the camera here, but he was dubbed "Black Jack" for his dark moods and fierce temper.

The sight of Jack Brabham on the grid at the 1961 Indianapolis 500 is amusing even now, so just imagine how outlandish it was to the Americans, his Cooper dwarfed by the giant roadsters. Stranger still, the engine was in the back... Jack said it was the prize money that drew him there, but it was also the encouragement of 1959 Indy 500 winner Rodger Ward. Fitting the race into his calendar was hard enough, but Jack qualified on the fifth row. Not surprisingly, his Cooper was down on power, but streets ahead in terms of manoeuvrability. Trying to save his tyres so that only two pitstops would be needed rather than three proved a mistake, as he did have to come in three times, and further time was lost with a wheel nut that had to be hammered on and off. Jack finished ninth and sowed the seeds for other rear-engined cars to tackle this bastion of conservatism.

When the 1.5-litre formula was introduced in 1961, Ferrari leapt to the fore. Ever shrewd, Jack saw the potential for production racing cars and formed Motor Racing Developments with Tauranac. The first Brabham made its debut in 1962, after he'd filled in with a Lotus.

Dan Gurney joined Jack and, although they won non-championship races at Solitude and Zeltweg, they didn't win a world championship round until the 1964 French Grand Prix, when Gurney triumphed. The demands of the business sent Jack into semi-retirement in 1965, but he returned in 1966 and, at Reims, finally won in a Brabham, going on to clinch his third title after bagging wins in the British, Dutch and German Grands Prix.

Runner-up to team-mate Denny Hulme in 1967, Jack signed Jochen Rindt for 1968, but there were problems with the Repco engine and Rindt left for Lotus. Jack was then joined by Jacky Ickx and, more important, Ford DFV engines for 1969. Jack won the non-championship International Trophy at Silverstone then broke an ankle when testing and had to miss three mid-season grands prix, but Ickx finished second overall to Jackie Stewart and was snapped up by Ferrari.

Jack was determined that 1970 would be his final year. It started with victory at Kyalami, but there was frustration at Monaco when he was pursued relentlessly by Rindt and went straight on at the final hairpin. He reversed out and finished a furious second. Then at Brands Hatch he ran out of fuel and again Rindt came past to win.

Jack retired at year's end and ran cars for Graham Hill and Tim Schenken in 1971 before selling up to Bernie Ecclestone. Further changes of ownership would follow before the team, still called Brabham, folded in 1992.

Jack's three sons, Geoff, Gary and David, were all successful racers, with David graduating to Formula One with Brabham, naturally, in 1990 then racing with Simtek before earning his living in sportscars. Gary also reached Formula One in 1990, but failed to qualify the hopeless Life F1 car. Geoff won title after title on the North American sportscar scene.

Now in his eighties, Jack isn't someone who likes to slow down, although the need for dialysis has kept him from driving racing cars as much as he would like on the historic scene.

TOP: Damon Hill made his Formula One debut with Brabham in 1992, in what would be the team's final year.

LEFT: Denny Hulme's 1967 title-winning Brabham BT24 is among the gems in the Donington Collection.

THE 1970s
SPECTACULAR RACING, TRAGIC CONSEQUENCES

The Ford DFV transformed Formula One, bringing in new teams, but it was still a dangerous sport as well as a glamorous one, and drivers were still meeting their deaths.

Jochen Rindt was the driver to beat in 1970. He won in Monaco in the Lotus 49 after Jack Brabham slid off on the final lap, before changing to Lotus's new 72 and winning four races in a row. Then, after engine failure at his home grand prix, he was killed in practice at Monza. Victory in the US Grand Prix by his replacement Emerson Fittipaldi ensured that Rindt's total couldn't be overhauled by Ferrari's Jacky Ickx. The season is also remembered for the arrival of March, with Jackie Stewart and Chris Amon filling the top two grid slots for the opening race. Sadly, Rindt wasn't the only driver to die, as the year also saw Bruce McLaren crashing when testing at Goodwood and de Tomaso racer Piers Courage burning to death at Zandvoort.

Ken Tyrrell's first self-made car was turned into a winner by Stewart in 1971, his six victories putting him way clear. March racer Ronnie Peterson was next best, despite failing to win a race. BRM did, and Peter Gethin's victory at Monza remains the closest in history, with the first five cars covered by 0.61 seconds.

Fittipaldi's black and gold Lotus 72 came on strong in 1972, and his five wins were enough to keep Stewart as runner-up, although the Scot's season was interrupted by a stomach ulcer. BRM took a surprise win in the rain at Monaco thanks to Jean-Pierre Beltoise, but this was to prove its last. Chris Amon was heading for victory in France in his Matra until a puncture thwarted this ever unlucky Kiwi.

Stewart was back to full strength in 1973 and raced to his third world title despite the best efforts of Fittipaldi. Having already decided to retire after the final race, the US Grand Prix at Watkins Glen, Stewart withdrew from it after his planned successor as Tyrrell team leader, François Cevert, crashed to his death in qualifying.

Formula One went through change in 1974, with no Stewart, Fittipaldi now in a McLaren and Ickx in his place at Lotus. The move proved shrewd for Fittipaldi, as the M23 was more advanced than the Lotus 72, and he and team-mate Denny Hulme set the ball rolling. Then Carlos

Reutemann showed that Brabham had found its feet again for the first time since its take-over by Bernie Ecclestone. However, Ferrari was finally back on song, as shown by a one-two for Niki Lauda and Clay Regazzoni at Jarama. Tyrrell also scored a one-two, at Anderstorp, with Scheckter pipping Patrick Depailler. Peterson kept the Lotus challenge going with three wins, but Fittipaldi, Regazzoni and Scheckter kept piling on the points until Fittipaldi was crowned.

Lauda turned Ferrari into an ever sharper tool in 1975, helping it to make its cars more reliable. He didn't win until the fifth round, but was in charge from then, his tranverse-gearboxed 312T the class of the field. The Spanish Grand Prix at Montjuich Park was a disaster when the barriers weren't strong enough to contain Rolf Stommelen's Hill and it killed five spectators. At Silverstone a downpour sent almost all the cars sliding off the track. But Lauda kept on winning and ended the year well clear of Fittipaldi. Notable one-off wins were scored by Carlos Pace for Brabham and Vittorio Brambilla for March, while James Hunt gave Hesketh its only victory.

Hunt was even bigger news in 1976 when he joined McLaren, Fittipaldi having chosen to driver for his brother Wilson's team. Lauda and Regazzoni set the initial pace, but Hunt hit form and it became a battle between him and Lauda. This was interrupted at the Nurburgring when Lauda crashed and, although pulled from the wreckage by three drivers, suffered terrible burns. Amazingly, he was racing again six weeks later, but he withdrew early in the final race in

ABOVE: Jochen Rindt was the first champion of the decade, but was crowned posthumously in 1970, beating Ferrari's Jacky Ickx (behind).

LEFT: Triple world champion Jackie Stewart always raced with his helmet sporting a royal Stewart tartan band.

RIGHT: Ferrari's Niki Lauda leads away at Zolder in 1976, chased by James Hunt's McLaren and Clay Regazzoni.

BELOW: Emerson Fittipaldi celebrates his first race as reigning world champion with another win for Lotus at Buenos Aires in 1973.

LEFT: The most distinctive car of the 1970s was the six-wheeled Tyrrell. This is Jody Scheckter driving it to victory in the 1976 Swedish GP at Anderstorp.

RIGHT: The Lotus 72 remains one of Formula One's classic shapes. This is Ronnie Peterson's 72E from 1974.

a downpour in Japan and Hunt took the title by a point.

The first new technology for a while came when Renault introduced turbo engines in 1977. Jean-Pierre Jabouille qualified only 21st at Silverstone, then retired, but it was a portent of things to come. The year belonged to Lauda and Ferrari, although Scheckter gave everyone a scare by winning the opening round for the new Wolf team and went on to finish as runner-up.

The other novelty in 1977 was "ground effects". Colin Chapman's Lotus 78 had its sidepods closed to the ground by skirts to channel more air under the car for extra downforce. Mario Andretti used this to win three times. Then its replacement, the 79, was another step forward in 1978. Brabham reckoned a fan car that sucked air out from underneath was a better interpretation, and Lauda won in Sweden, but the FIA outlawed it. Andretti was thus clear to dominate, but it was to turn into a dreadfully sad year for Lotus as his team-mate Peterson was killed in an accident off the startline in the Italian Grand Prix at Monza.

Ligier dominated the first two races in 1979 through Jacques Laffite and later won at Jarama with Depailler, but it was Ferrari who came on strong with Scheckter and Gilles Villeneuve winning six grands prix. Renault scored its breakthrough win through Jabouille, while the second half of the year was Williams territory as Alan Jones won four times. However, Scheckter did just enough to be champion.

ABOVE: Wide, slick (i.e. treadless) Goodyear tyres were used by all of the teams through the mid-1970s.

LEFT: Lotus introduced ground effects in 1977 and Mario Andretti raced to the 1978 title, winning here in France.

ENCLOSURE 1: The late Roger Williamson's driving licence.

ENCLOSURE 2: Roger Williamson's British Automobile Racing Club membership card.

ENCLOSURE 3: Roger Williamson's competition licence.

ENCLOSURE 4: Roger Williamson's blood donor card from the year that he was killed, 1973.

THE DEATH OF ROGER WILLIAMSON

One of the saddest incidents in a decade that contained a few was the death of Roger WIlliamson at Zandvoort. In only his second grand prix, this hugely promising 25-year-old English racer crashed his Wheatcroft Racing March coming up to Scheivlak after what is thought to have been a tyre failure. The barrier he hit simply acted as a launch pad and fired him back across the track, his car coming to rest upside down, on fire. Roger couldn't get out, and the drama turned into a crisis as a nearby fire tender wouldn't travel up the grass verge against the flow of traffic to help him. Worse still, the marshals weren't up to the job and only fellow racer David Purley went in to help him, earning the George Medal for his brave but sadly unsuccessful attempts to extract poor Roger. It was a tragic, unnecessary waste of a keen and enormously talented racer.

NIKI LAUDA
BRAVEST OF THE BRAVE

This was the driver who dragged Ferrari out of a hole, was nearly burned to death, fought back to be champion, started his own airline and then made another triumphant return.

One of the bravest and most intelligent drivers ever to drive a Formula One car, Niki Lauda knew when to say "enough". That was in 1976, when the defending World Champion pulled out of the finale in pouring rain in Japan. It was just 12 weeks after he had received the last rites following his terrifying crash at the Nurburgring, and it allowed James Hunt to take the title.

Being taken to the German Grand Prix by friends in 1966 was a life-changing experience for Niki. He was 17 at the time and it made up his mind that he too would like to race. To counter opposition from his wealthy Viennese parents, he told them that the racing Mini Cooper in their garage was simply being stored for a friend. They fell for it and Niki began his competition career in hillclimbs in 1968. Then, with no money forthcoming from his family, it was only when he took a bank loan that Niki was able to proceed, the manager reckoning that Niki's family were wealthy enough to pay up if he defaulted...

Niki had already advanced to single-seaters in 1969, racing in Formula Vee, then Formula Three and even in a Porsche 908 sportscar, when he used the loan to buy himself a place in the March Formula Two team in 1971. It was easy to knock him as just another rich kid, but this was shown to be unfair when he had to be given the "slow" signal at Rouen to prevent him beating team-mate Ronnie Peterson.

Niki made his Formula One debut that same year at the Österreichring and tried to buy a March Formula One ride for 1972, but the bank stopped his loan. Niki restructured the loan and went ahead, but the March was

terribly uncompetitive. Luckily, he was offered the third BRM for 1973 and was soon matching Clay Regazzoni and Jean-Pierre Beltoise, both already grand prix winners, then outpacing them. BRM even started to pay him. When he led in the wet in Canada, Ferrari paid attention.

By 1974, Niki was with the Italian team and was a revelation. He was second on his debut. Then, starting from pole position more often than not, he began to look like a potential champion. He won at Jarama and Zandvoort and dominated at Brands Hatch until a puncture forced him to pit, only to find the exit blocked. Other problems wrecked the second half of the campaign and he dropped to fourth.

In 1975, Niki was definitely the main man in a new and improved Ferrari, racing to wins in Monaco, Belgium, Sweden, France and the USA, and a reduction in the number of mechanical failures helped him be crowned World Champion.

Back-to-back titles looked to be coming Niki's way in 1976 as he made a storming start to the season. Then, following his fifth win at the British Grand Prix after James Hunt was disqualified, Niki crashed at the Nurburgring and his car caught fire. He was pulled out by four fellow drivers, terribly burnt and with seared lungs. Yet six weeks later he was back, racing to a heroic fourth at Monza. A strong run by James Hunt threatened his lead and, in the last race at Fuji, Niki pulled out after a lap in appalling

ABOVE: Niki Lauda, trailing team-mate Jean-Pierre Beltoise, found his feet with BRM in 1973 before joining Ferrari.

LEFT: Lauda's team leadership skills became apparent when he joined Ferrari in 1974 and he raced to his first world title in 1975, taking five wins.

BELOW: Sporting his trademark cap and sunglasses, Lauda returned to racing scarred but not bowed by his fiery accident in the 1976 German GP.

conditions, unable to blink in the spray due to his burns, and so lost the title to Hunt by a point.

Ferrari's decision to make Carlos Reutemann team leader in 1977 prompted Niki to rediscover his winning ways. Victories at Kyalami, Zandvoort and Hockenheim – given the German Grand Prix after Lauda's crash proved that the Nurburgring was too dangerous – combined with seven other top-three finishes, were enough for his second title.

Niki now decided to quit Ferrari for Brabham, but this didn't pay off as he ranked only fourth, the highlight for him being victory in Sweden in Brabham's immediately outlawed "fan car". Then it fell apart, his 1979 campaign turning into a disaster as Alfa Romeo's V12 proved most unreliable in the back of his BT48. Niki quit at the penultimate grand prix, saying that he no longer wanted to "drive a racing car around in circles".

The trouble was that Niki was wrong – he couldn't stay away. Even the satisfaction of running his increasingly successful charter airline was not enough to keep him out of the cockpit in 1982. He didn't return with Ferrari or Brabham, but with McLaren. The sure touch was still there and Niki won at Long Beach and Brands Hatch, which was as much as he could expect as the team didn't have a turbo engine. This didn't arrive until the closing races of 1983, but the TAG turbo engine was so good that Niki won five times in 1984 to pip team-mate Alain Prost by half a point to be champion for a third time.

Niki knew he wouldn't be able to beat Prost again, and his highlight in 1985 was his final win at Zandvoort before he retired for good. Well, retired from "driving around in circles" at least...

ABOVE: This is the helmet livery that Lauda sported when he returned to Formula One with McLaren in the mid-1980s.

LEFT: After quittng Ferrari, Lauda joined Brabham for 1978, and he won the Swedish GP at Anderstorp in the only appearance for the infamous BT46B fan car.

BELOW: Winning the 1984 British GP for McLaren at Brands Hatch helped Lauda move towards his third world title.

NIKI LAUDA AS A TEAM BOSS

Some former Formula One racers take the route into team management when they've retired from the cockpit, feeling that their success as drivers will guarantee that they can reproduce the wins from the pitwall. Actually, it is often not so much a love of being in charge of an enterprise that drives them, more the fear of not having any involvement any more. Perhaps as a result of this, few succeed. As one of the more cerebral drivers, it came as no surprise that Lauda gave it a go. After all, he already had business experience from running his own, successful charter airline. So he leapt at the chance to rejoin Ferrari in a consultancy role in 1992 that continued through until 1999. He then took over Ford's Premier Performance Division (including Cosworth and Jaguar Racing) in 2001, and his involvement with Jaguar Racing increased after he removed Bobby Rahal from running it... Then, caught out by internal politics, he left his post at the end of 2002.

UNITED STATES GP
FOLLOW THE YELLOW BRICK ROAD

This is a nomad among races, always on the move apart from a lengthy spell at Watkins Glen and shorter ones at Long Beach and the Indianapolis Motor Speedway.

The United States Grand Prix is one that is incredibly important to Formula One, but has never really had a home to call its own, and now it has been dropped altogether, which certainly doesn't delight the Formula One teams' sponsors. And, with NASCAR stock car racing growing more popular and more powerful with every year, there is a major fight to get it back on board.

For the first 10 years of the World Championship, the Indianapolis 500 – America's most important open-wheel race – was included in the calendar, although few European drivers entered. Ironically, it was only really after it had been dropped that Formula One drivers started making forays there, eager to pick up the considerable prize money. Their involvement transformed the race, their belief that small (and rear-engined) was beautiful flying in the face of the received wisdom that the cars must be big roadsters. No sooner had Jim Clark given them all a scare when he placed second – and he would have won the race if Parnelli Jones's car had been black-flagged for spilling oil – than the Indy designers starting working on cars similar to his little Lotus. Clark

then hit gold in 1965, and Graham Hill gave the Lola marque its first win there in 1966. However, by this time, the actual United States Grand Prix had been on a bit of a nationwide tour.

It started at pancake-flat Sebring in Florida in 1959, then crossed to the other seaboard for a race at undulating Riverside in California the following year. Finally it found a home as Watkins Glen in upstate New York welcomed it in 1961. The weather could be mixed as autumn fell, but the race on this up-and-down circuit was seldom less than exciting, with Clark and Hill taking three wins apiece between 1962 and 1967. Both had even more reason to be pleased than normal, as the prize cheque was not to be sniffed at and certainly helped with the team's budget. It eventually lost the race after its 1980 running, when Alan Jones was in his pomp for Williams. Before that, sadly, Watkins Glen had been the scene of two fatal accidents in 1973 and 1974 that claimed the lives of François Cevert then Helmuth Koinigg in extremely similar circumstances.

In 1976, America began hosting a second grand prix each year, at Long Beach in California (see sidebar). This ran until 1983, with the US Grand Prix effectively being renamed the Las Vegas Grand Prix in 1981 and 1982 when a track was laid out in the grounds of the Caesar's Palace casino in this gambling city. Dallas also had

BELOW LEFT: The first US GP was held at Sebring, Florida, as the last race of the 1959 season. Stirling Moss (7) led away from champion-elect Jack Brabham (8), but the race was won by Bruce McLaren from the fourth row.

ABOVE: The US GP soon moved, crossing Riverside in California, for 1960. However, it also was only for one year. Jack Brabham led for part of the race, but Stirling Moss, in a privately-entered Lotus took pole and won the race.

BELOW: Jackie Stewart won the 1972 US GP at Watkins Glen, but would withdraw before the start of the 1973 race, following the death of team-mate François Cevert during practice.

a crack in 1984, but the Texan city had two problems – a lack of interest locally and a circuit that was breaking up – and it was a one-off.

Detroit, home of the US automotive business, was a more logical and interested home for Formula One from 1982 to 1988, with a race downtown, alongside a river. Fittingly, the final win for Ford's Cosworth DFV engine came in Motor City when Michele Alboreto guided his Tyrrell home in front in 1983. The racing at Detroit was often punctuated by cars hitting the concrete barriers, mainly owing to the preponderance of 90-degree bends combined with a notoriously bumpy surface, but Ayrton Senna clearly loved it as he won here three years in a row. The race then found itself on the move again, to another street circuit, this time in Phoenix, Arizona, but it was business as usual for Senna, who won two of the three races held there.

From 1992 to 1999, the USA was without a stop for the Formula One circus, but a tailor-made circuit was built at the Indianapolis Motor Speedway, combining the main straight and one of the banked corners with a snaking infield section. The advantage was that the IMS can hold enormous crowds. The disadvantage was that the racing was seldom as close or spectacular as it is there in oval trim. Then, crime of crimes, all but six cars pulled out just before the start in 2005 in a stand to highlight concerns about the safety of Michelin's tyres after Ralf Schumacher had one go in practice and it put his Williams into the wall.

The American fans felt cheated and, in a market that was already increasingly unsure about Formula One, the US Grand Prix was on rocky ground once more. So much so that the grand prix wasn't held in 2008 and it isn't on the calendar for 2009.

There have been numerous proposals for a new home for the US Grand Prix, some on street circuits in city centres, others on flowing road courses out in the sticks, but nobody has ever really found the right formula for this very different racing market. A return to Indianapolis was not the right answer, as the cars look wrong there, dwarfed by the facilities. However, F1 is having another roll of the dice in the USA as a new circuit has been built outside Austin, in Texas, with a classical road racing style that ought to capture the American public's imagination once more.

LONG BEACH

Monaco is the jewel in Formula One's crown and pretty much always has been, but America wanted a jewel of its own. Enter Chris Pook, an American-domiciled British promoter. He had convinced the Californian retirement city of Long Beach to host a race meeting in 1975 to spice up its image. Having seen that it worked, Formula One went there the following year for a second American round in addition to the grand prix at Watkins Glen. The race, known as the United States Grand Prix West, was won by Ferrari's Clay Regazzoni, who was best around the steeply undulating top part of the circuit with its flat-out blast along the waterfront past the permanently berthed liner *Queen Mary*, now a hotel. Unfortunately Regazzoni was crippled when he crashed at the end of Shoreline Drive in 1980. The grand prix kept going there until 1983, when John Watson scored a famous charge from 22nd place to victory.

LEFT: Detroit's office blocks provide an imposing backdrop to the 1982 grand prix, a race won from 17th on the grid by McLaren's John Watson (red and white).

RIGHT: Mario Andretti provided the American fans with a home winner in 1977 on Formula One's second visit to the streets of Long Beach.

BELOW RIGHT: When all but six cars withdrew before the start of the 2005 US GP, the fans were rightly furious.

ENCLOSURE: A poster for the 1970 United States Grand Prix back-to-back with a poster for the 1974 United States Grand Prix, also at Watkins Glen.

FERRARI
LEGEND OF THE PRANCING HORSE

There is no more famous name in motor racing. Enzo Ferrari's influence is clear from the 1920s until his death in 1988, and his team goes on to even greater heights.

LEFT: Alberto Ascari's light blue 1950s' open-faced helmet is one of many "lids" on display in the Donington Collection.

BELOW: Michael Schumacher turned the team into title challengers again and landed the first of his five titles with Ferrari in 2000.

BOTTOM LEFT: Enzo Ferrari (centre) poses with drivers Luigi Villoresi (left) and Alberto Ascari (right), both of whom drove in the team's Formula One debut in 1950, but he cared more for his cars than the drivers.

BELOW: The Sharknose Ferrari was the class of 1961 after a change in the rules introduced the 1.5 litre formula. Sadly, Wolfgang von Trips was killed at Monza.

No team in Formula One excites greater passion. Show anyone a red car with a black prancing horse on a yellow badge and they will know it's a Ferrari. Its sportscars are lusted after by car nuts the world over. To them, Formula One is Ferrari versus the rest. No other team has raced in every year of the World Championship and had a grand prix (the San Marino) created so that its fans – the tifosi (fanatics) – could have a second annual dose of the magic.

Founded by Enzo Ferrari, this team was nearly called Mutina, the Latin name for his home town of Modena, which would have carried the dreams just as well. Enzo had been a racer in the 1920s, then ran Alfa Romeos from 1929, including the works team from 1930 to 1939, when he was paid to stay away from racing for four years. After the Second World War, he bounced back, teaming up with designer Gioacchino Colombo, moving from Modena to Maranello and building the first Ferrari grand prix car in 1948. The 125 was powered by a supercharged V12 after Enzo had been inspired by photos of a 12-cylinder Packard at the Indy 500. Twelve-cylinder engines were central to his cars until 1995, except when rules dictated otherwise.

Enzo was an excellent organizer and his love for his team was total, but the cars came first, with the drivers just part of the equation, apart from an exceptional few. For someone who felt so deeply about his cars, he was notoriously unsentimental about them, and throughout the 1960s they were often chopped up after they had been superseded...

When the World Championship began in 1950, with Alfa Romeo dominant, the works team joined in at the second round, with Alberto Ascari finishing second. Trounced in the Swiss GP, things improved only after Aurelio Lampredi got rid of the supercharger and launched the 375, helping Ascari finish second at Monza. The all-important first win came at the 1951 British Grand Prix, with Jose Froilan Gonzalez at the wheel, followed by Ascari winning the next two, and the team hasn't looked back. Indeed, in 58 campaigns to the end of 2008, Ferrari has won 209 times from 776 starts, taken 16 constructors' titles and 15 drivers' titles.

With Alfa Romeo gone and a new set of regulations for 1952, it was a Ferrari whitewash, with Piero Taruffi winning the opener, then Ascari taking control to win the next nine races to wrap up the 1952 and 1953 titles, and Mike Hawthorn and Giuseppe Farina also getting in on the act.

Then came another rule change and Ferrari struggled against Maserati then Mercedes until it bought Lancia's D50s and ran them in 1956, a year that saw Peter Collins becoming a rare Enzo favourite after his own son Dino died, and Juan Manuel Fangio becoming World Champion.

After a winless 1957, Ferrari bounced back in 1958 and Hawthorn just held off the Vanwall onslaught to win the title. Despite the evidence that rear-engined cars were the way to go, Ferrari kept on with its front-engined racers until 1960. Luckily, the change to a

1.5-litre formula for 1961 was good to Ferrari. But the British teams got their act together, and after a host of its leading personnel left in 1962 Ferrari fell away until John Surtees guided it to the title in 1964. Problems then mounted as Surtees walked out in 1966, Lorenzo Bandini crashed fatally at Monaco in 1967, and the arrival of Ford's DFV engine left it floundering.

Money troubles were alleviated in 1969 when Fiat bought Ferrari, and Jacky Ickx challenged strongly for the 1970 world title in his 312B. But Ferrari lost its way again until Niki Lauda sorted it out in 1974 and claimed titles in 1975 and 1977. However, even he wasn't made to feel comfortable by Enzo after his comeback from the injuries he received when he crashed in the 1976 German Grand Prix. Success finally returned to Ferrari in 1979 when Jody Scheckter and Enzo's other favourite, Gilles Villeneuve, led the way. The following year, Ferrari ranked 10th...

Ferrari's form didn't improve until it brought in Harvey Postlethwaite for 1982 to focus on chassis design. By then, McLaren and Williams had got into their stride, and Ferrari only became a top team again when Jean Todt arrived in 1993, five years after Enzo's death, sorted out the internal structure and signed Michael Schumacher for 1996. The team was transformed, becoming more cosmopolitan. Gone was the brio, but in its place was a run of five straight drivers' titles for Schumacher from 2000 to 2004, then one for Kimi Raikkonen in 2007 although Felipe Massa fell agonisingly short in 2008 and Fernando Alonso lost out in the 2010 finale, with the team now under Stefano Domenicali's control.

LEFT: Ferrari team principal Stefano Domenicali and Fernando Alonso demonstrate their rapport in 2011.

BELOW: Ferrari's 312B was a winner in the hands of Jacky Ickx and Clay Regazzoni in the second half of the 1970 season.

FERRARI'S MARANELLO HQ

Anyone fortunate enough to visit the ultra-modern McLaren Technology Centre will wonder, on seeing Maranello from its front gate for the first time, what all the fuss is about. It looks like a remnant of the industrial architecture that spread across Italy's northern plains in the 1970s. It might even be a plastics factory, yet it has a heart and the patina of an incredible history. Inside, everything is state-of-the-art, as you would expect from a team that has always built not only its own chassis but its own engines too, not to forget its mouthwatering range of road-going sportscars. Its Fiorano test circuit was built at Maranello in 1972, close enough to the main offices for Enzo to have to close his windows if he was having a meeting. Opposite the gates, Ferrari has built a gallery to show off the great cars from its illustrious past.

ALAIN PROST
ALWAYS IN CONTROL

Known as "The Professor", Alain never looked particularly fast, but four world titles proved incontrovertibly that he really was, as well as being an extremely wily operator.

LEFT: Alain Prost (left) chats to compatriot Didier Pironi in 1980, his debut year in Formula One with McLaren.

FAR LEFT: Prost's white and blue helmet sports the logos of McLaren's late 1980s sponsors Marlboro and Boss.

Alain Prost is almost a forgotten man among Formula One's legends. He has four world titles to his name, exceeded only by Juan Manuel Fangio and Michael Schumacher, and only Schumacher has passed his tally of 51 wins, yet somehow he never won the hearts of the public.

Political manipulation was why, with Prost not endearing himself by trying his utmost to ensure that he had the best equipment, even if that created an uncomfortable situation within his own team. This marred his years in the late 1980s as team-mate to Ayrton Senna at McLaren, and few were surprised that, when Alain turned to team ownership in 1997, it didn't work out.

Out on the circuit, Prost was magnificent, despite his way of making his driving undramatic and thus look slow from the sidelines, much as his racing heroes Jim Clark and Jackie Stewart did. If there was a way to beat a driver/car combination of similar speed by tactical nous, you always felt that Alain would do it; hence his nickname "The Professor".

After having a go on a kart track during a family holiday at the age of 14, Alain started racing karts, but he was also playing a lot of football, which is how his famously bent nose got broken. Alain very nearly took the football route, but winning the karting junior world title in 1973 changed all that and he graduated to car racing. After being crowned as French Formula Renault champion in 1976, he won the European crown the following year, then stepped up to Formula Three and really made his mark by winning the European and French Formula Three titles in 1979, with his most high-profile win coming in the Monaco Grand Prix support race.

Formula One beckoned, and Prost joined McLaren for 1980, when the team was at a low ebb. However, he outpaced experienced team-mate John Watson and finished sixth on his debut in Argentina. Fifth followed in Brazil, after which he broke his wrist in South Africa.

LOSING THE 1983 FINALE

It was as if written for a movie: Alain Prost, son of France, was going to guide Renault, team of France, to their first world titles. The setting was the South African Grand Prix, the season finale, and Prost had a two-point lead over Nelson Piquet. Alain had been telling Renault that it wasn't a cert, but the management didn't appear to listen and flew journalists out to witness this double triumph. Piquet qualified second behind Patrick Tambay's Ferrari but was confident as his Brabham-BMW was easily faster than Prost's Renault which was starting three places further back. Starting with a light fuel load, Piquet got the jump on Tambay and led away, while Prost passed Tambay then Andrea de Cesaris for third. But he himself was passed by Niki Lauda. Things weren't looking good, and when he pitted for fuel he hopped out, knowing that his turbo was on the verge of failing. Piquet would only have to finish third to take the crown, which he did.

LEFT: Prost's Renault RE30 is challenged by John Watson's McLaren at Dijon-Prenois in 1981, but he held on to win.

Anxious to become a winner, Alain joined Renault for 1981 and was on the podium at only his third attempt, in Argentina. Better was to follow and Alain won, most fittingly, his home grand prix. Success in two more grands prix left him fifth overall, but only seven points behind the World Champion. He went one place better in 1982 in another incredibly close title race. The fact that he had won the opening two races had suggested that it would be his year, but after that he failed to win again.

Four wins in 1983 was better and he led on points going to the final round (see sidebar), but he ended the year as runner-up to Nelson Piquet and was fired by Renault for speaking out, so he found himself back at McLaren for 1984. This was the start of his greatest period.

In an incredible year Prost won seven grands prix, but it still was not enough to be champion and he was runner-up to his team-mate, Niki Lauda, by half a point. Fortunately, everything went his way in 1985, with wins at Rio de Janeiro, Monaco, Silverstone, the Österreichring and Monza helping Alain to the title. In brilliant form, he made it two titles on the trot in 1986, but this was far tighter and he only came out on top after a twist of fate in a three-way shoot-out in Adelaide, crossing the finish line with a fuel gauge long since reading empty.

The arrival of Ayrton Senna as a team-mate at McLaren in 1988 made life interesting, as Prost had become accustomed to being top dog in the team, lording it over first Keke Rosberg then Stefan Johansson. Now, matched for pace, he had to play politics to keep the Brazilian behind him and it got nasty, particularly when Senna took the drivers' title.

The 1989 title went Alain's way, but it took a collision with

Senna in the Japanese Grand Prix to wrap it up. Prost quit McLaren for Ferrari, but sadly the tension simmered on and Senna took his revenge at the same venue, simply driving Prost off the track to ensure that he became champion rather than Alain. With no wins forthcoming in 1991 and Alain unhappy about the politics at Ferrari, he spoke out once too often and was fired even before the final round.

Life without racing didn't hold much allure, and Alain was back in 1993, having taken Williams's lead seat from Nigel Mansell. It was the car to have and he waltzed to the title ahead of Senna by taking seven wins. However, news that Senna was to join him led to Prost resigning.

Afterwards, Alain took that fateful dive into team management when he bought Ligier and renamed it Prost for 1997. It didn't go well, the team sliding further down the order each year, until in 2001 it folded, its best result having been Jarno Trulli's second place in the topsy-turvy 1999 European Grand Prix.

THE 1980s
NEW KIDS ON THE BLOCK

Two British teams – McLaren and Williams – arrived when Ford DFVs made Formula One affordable and blossomed to dominate the 1980s with a new group of drivers.

Before 1980, McLaren had won one constructors' title, Williams none. By 1990, they had five and four respectively. No driver was dominant in the early part of the decade, yet by its end three heavyweights battled it out: Nelson Piquet, Alain Prost and Ayrton Senna.

Those who say that politics should have no place in sport are right, but, sadly, the more money involved in a sport, the more politics intrude. With Formula One starting to be big business in 1980, a clash was inevitable. The season had kicked off with Alan Jones and Williams showing they were the combination to beat. It was Renault, however, with its turbo engine producing ever more power, that took the next two races through René Arnoux, after which Piquet won for Brabham at Long Beach. Then Didier Pironi won at Zolder and Jones's team-mate Carlos Reutemann at Monaco, but it got messy in Spain when the manufacturer teams – Alfa Romeo, Ferrari and Renault – withdrew. At the time, FOCA (the Formula One Constructors' Association) was engaged in a long-running powerplay with the sport's governing body. This withdrawal after the race organizer had sided with FOCA, rendered the event ineligible for championship points. Jones won easily and would go on to be World Champion.

It came down to a three-way shoot-out at Las Vegas in 1981 between Jones, team-mate Reutemann and Piquet. Jones won the race, but Reutemann slid ever further backwards to an inexplicable eighth place, letting Piquet take the crown with fifth place.

The FISA v. FOCA wars resurfaced in 1982 after Prost had won the first two races for Renault, victory in the second race coming after Piquet and Williams driver Keke Rosberg had been disqualified for being underweight. They had been exploiting a loophole that let teams top up their brake cooling tanks after a race to bring them back above the minimum weight, and the ramifications of this were made plain at the San Marino Grand Prix. Between the incident and the reaction, Niki Lauda had scored his first win on his return with McLaren. Then came the race at Imola, which the FOCA teams boycotted, leaving 14 cars, of which only the Renaults and Ferraris were competitive. Engine failure accounted for both Renaults, leaving Ferrari free to win. The trouble was that Pironi went back on a pre-race agreement with Gilles Villeneuve that whoever was leading at the start of the final lap should win. In qualifying for the next race at Zolder, Villeneuve, still livid, was trying to beat Pironi's time when he fatally clipped another car.

Sadly, his wasn't the only death, as Pironi stalled at the start in Canada and Riccardo Paletti was killed when he slammed into the back of the Ferrari. Pironi was not to escape the year unharmed either, his career ending when he smashed his legs at Hockenheim. On the plus side, Brabham added interest by introducing refuelling at the Austrian Grand Prix, meaning that it could run its cars with half a fuel load. It worked for Riccardo Patrese and he resumed in the lead, only for

TOP: Australian Alan Jones was the first world champion of the 1980s, winning five races for Frank Williams's team.

ABOVE LEFT: Ferrari superstar Gilles Villeneuve's death in qualifying for the 1982 Belgian GP at Zolder shook Formula One to the core, as he'd been a driver who inspired.

LEFT: Brabham's Nelson Piquet (left), Riccardo Patrese and Andrea de Cesaris (right) celebrate at Kyalami in 1983 after the Italian had won the season finale and the Brazilian had claimed the second of his three World Championship titles.

his engine to fail. Overall, it was a year of poor reliability, and Rosberg took the title despite winning just once.

The 1983 season was less complicated and the title should have been Prost's, but Brabham was more competitive than Renault at the end of the season and Piquet pipped him at the final race when Prost's turbo failed.

It looked as though 1984 might belong to Renault, with Derek Warwick set to win the opener until his RE50's suspension broke. This handed victory to Prost for a triumphant return to McLaren. He would go on to win six more, but team-mate Lauda took the title by half a point.

Prost hit back in 1985 to take his first title, with Michele Alboreto best of the rest for Ferrari. Prost did it again in 1986, but this was more of a challenge as it looked to be going Nigel Mansell's way after a strong mid-season run in his Williams-Honda brought five wins. He headed to the finale in the lead, but Prost took the crown (see sidebar).

Williams redoubled its efforts for 1987, and again Prost was the thorn in their side. Then, with the active suspension working on his Lotus, Senna came into the reckoning, but Piquet raced to his third title, much to Mansell's chagrin. Mansell did have the delight, however, of pulling off the move of the year on Piquet in the British Grand Prix.

Taking on the Honda engines Williams had enjoyed in 1987, McLaren trounced the opposition in 1988. But they, like Williams, had two drivers with no time for each other. It came to a head at Estoril when Prost tried to pass Senna, who was leading, and Senna all but squeezed him into the pitwall. After winning in Japan, Senna was champion for the first time with just one race to go. Prost struck back in 1989, but it again went right the way to the end, with Prost taking Senna off in Japan.

LEFT: Nigel Mansell's patriotically-coloured helmet design summed up what drove him towards his 31 grand prix wins.

RIGHT: Nigel Mansell, Alain Prost, Nelson Piquet, Keke Rosberg and Patrick Tambay lead the chasing pack behind Ayrton Senna early in the 1986 Hungarian GP.

BELOW RIGHT: Alain Prost (middle) won the 1984 Portuguese GP, although second place was enough to give Niki Lauda (left) the title, but only by half a point.

ABOVE: This Goodyear Eagle tyre sports the grooved tread required for racing in the rain when slicks wouldn't do.

BELOW: Patrick Tambay used this turbocharged Renault RE50 to finish second in the French GP in 1984, helping the team to rank fifth overall in the constructors' championship.

WILLIAMS
DETERMINATION TO SUCCEED

Frank Williams dreamt of Formula One glory for years, but it was only when he teamed up with Patrick Head in the late 1970s that the grand prix wins started flowing.

It's said that from little acorns oak trees grow, and in motor sport this was never more true than of Williams, a team that ranks behind only Ferrari and McLaren in its success.

Frank Williams was filled with determination when he turned his back on being a racing driver and started running cars for others. The trouble was, everything he did in his early days was hand-to-mouth. He was seen as a joke, mad to be trying to take on the big boys, but he persevered, and those who derided him had to watch as this ugly duckling turned into a swan.

Frank ran a car in Formula Three for former team-mate Piers Courage in 1967. They advanced to Formula Two in 1968, with future FIA president Max Mosley being run from mid-season. It was decided to enter Courage in Formula One in a Brabham in 1969 and this was validated when he came second in Monaco and picked up another second place in the US Grand Prix. Frank hooked up with sportscar manufacturer de Tomaso for 1970, and this could have been his ticket to the stars, but Courage crashed to his death at Zandvoort and de Tomaso quit. Frank then ran a March for Henri Pescarolo. For 1972, the Politoys toy company asked him to build a car, but Pescarolo wrecked this on its debut and spent the rest of the year crashing the team's March.

The Iso-Rivolta sportscar company wanted to try Formula One in 1973, and driver Nanni Galli helped finance the Iso Williams but left after five grands prix, after which Howden Ganley did little better. Quit? No chance. Frank was back in 1974, the cars now rebadged as Williams. Arturo Merzario arrived with Marlboro money, but this departed at the end of the year. Luckily, Jacques Lafitte scored a second place in the 1975 German Grand Prix. Then Frank ran a Hesketh for Walter Wolf Racing in 1976, and the team was all set for 1977, with a new car for Jody Scheckter,

when Frank was told that he wouldn't be going to the opening race, so he quit and ran a March instead for Patrick Neve.

This at last was the start of something big, as Frank formed Williams Grand Prix Engineering with Patrick Head, and money from sponsor Saudia enabled Head to design the FW06. It was a step up and few teams have made such an immediate impact as this, with Alan Jones fourth on only the car's third outing, later finishing second in the US Grand Prix.

Head's FW07 was a masterpiece. Clay Regazzoni gave the team its first win in the 1979 British Grand Prix – as a patriot, Frank loved that – and then Jones won four of the next five races. The following year he

TOP RIGHT: Frank Williams (left) gets feedback from his first charge, Piers Courage, in 1970. It was a relationship that came to a sudden, tragic end at Zandvoort later that season.

ABOVE: The helmet worn by Keke Rosberg, who drove for Williams from his title-winning year, 1982, through to 1985, winning one race each year.

BELOW: The first grand prix victory for Williams Grand Prix Engineering came in the 1979 British GP at Silverstone, courtesy of Clay Regazzoni.

ALAN JONES

Having watched his father win the Australian Grand Prix in 1959, Alan decided to go racing in England in 1967, at the age of 20, but couldn't afford it. Three years later, he financed his Formula Three by selling used cars. He was runner-up in 1973, and Harry Stiller entered Alan in Formula One in 1975 with a Hesketh. Graham Hill snapped him up to replace the injured Rolf Stommelen. Alan drove for Surtees in 1976, then landed a drive with Shadow in 1977 after Tom Pryce was killed and won the Austrian Grand Prix. Moving to Williams for 1978 (below), Alan peaked with second, then won four grands prix in 1979. A lack of reliability left him third overall. No such mistakes were made in 1980, when five wins helped Alan take a title that he came close to retaining in 1981. Alan quit after winning the last race in Las Vegas, made a brief return for Arrows in 1983 and a full-time one with Haas Lola.

more determined, Frank pressed on and he guided the team back to the top. Renault power made the team more competitive again, Adrian Newey designed the brilliant FW14, and Mansell dominated 1992 to become champion with five races still to run...

Rosberg said once that his only crime at Williams was "not being Alan Jones". Well, Frank showed more of the same when he responded to Mansell's title by not re-signing him. Alain Prost took his place and waltzed to his fourth title, and the team's sixth. Then, scared that Frank was signing Ayrton Senna, he quit. Damon Hill was another to experience harsh management during his title year in 1996. The team was bigger than its drivers. Before that, however, the team had its darkest hour at Imola in 1994 when Senna crashed to his death.

Jacques Villeneuve was champion in 1997, before BMW joined forces in 2000. The wins began again in 2001 through Ralf Schumacher and Juan Pablo Montoya, leading to second place in the 2002 and 2003 constructors' tables, but the team fell back, losing further ground when BMW left and it had to run Cosworth engines in 2006. An engine deal with Toyota ought to have put Williams back on track, but a lack of finance compared to the big hitters makes it ever more difficult but a deal to run Renault engines again for 2012 ought to give the team the boost its needs to get out of the midfield and back to the front.

LEFT: Patrick Head and Rubens Barrichello seem in good cheer in 2011, but their results did not offer much to smile about.

BELOW: Jacques Villeneuve made a major splash by leading Damon Hill, and the grand prix, on his Formula One debut in Melbourne in 1996.

BOTTOM: Nigel Mansell's 1986 Williams-Honda FW11, a car that would have taken him to the title, but for a tyre blow-out in the final race.

became champion, while further points from Carlos Reutemann helped the team to its first constructors' title. Williams had arrived.

Reutemann was unsettled by the team's love of Jones, and 1981 was uncomfortable. Reutemann crumpled in the finale and blew his title shot, but Jones made sure that he won his last race before retirement.

Keke Rosberg grabbed the drivers' title in 1982, but the team's lack of a turbocharged engine was starting to hurt and, apart from an inspired win at Monaco, 1983 was a holding year. Then Frank got his hands on Honda engines and, once their power delivery was tamed, the team started winning again. Nigel Mansell and Nelson Piquet were the feisty pairing for 1986 and 1987, with 18 wins and two constructors' titles, but only one drivers' crown, for Piquet in 1987.

Amid all this glory, Frank's life was transformed when he broke his neck in a road accident before the start of the 1986 season, leaving hIm wheelchair-bound. Slowed in body, but perhaps even

MONACO GRAND PRIX
JEWEL IN THE CROWN

Its confines, which were acceptable in the 1920s, were outrageous by the 1980s, and yet the race is still the first one marked on the World Championship calendar.

K nown as a millionaires' playground, this tiny principality on the Mediterranean coast encircled by France is best known for its grand prix, an event that flouts pretty much every rule thrown at other venues, but it remains the most important grand prix of all, by far.

Monaco has hosted a grand prix since 1929, when the mysterious "W. Williams" won in a Bugatti. Four years later it looked as if Achille Varzi or Tazio Nuvolari would die racing around the streets – they diced until the engine on Nuvolari's Alfa Romeo blew, leaving Varzi to win for Bugatti.

There have been changes to the layout, but not many, as the shape of the circuit is dictated by the narrow streets on which it must run. A swimming pool forced the insertion of esses along the harbour front, the original Gasworks hairpin has been turned into a tight left followed by a

right-hand hairpin, La Rascasse, and the hotel under which it tunnels has trebled in size. The rest is pretty much as it has always been.

The reason that Monaco is so important is that it is the place where the sponsors want to see and be seen, the lure of the casino and parties on yachts all adding to its allure. That it's incredibly inconvenient for those actually working on the cars has always been seen as a price worth paying. It was only recently that they were provided with pit garages rather than something closer in size to a cupboard, an inconvenience made all the worse by the paddock being reached only by a footbridge when the track was open.

One thing that has been clear since that first grand prix in 1929 is that the merest slip-up can lead to a clash with something solid, and a car pitched sideways can block the track. Take the first World Championship event held here in 1950, when Giuseppe Farina spun on the opening lap and nine other cars were caught out behind him. Juan Manuel Fangio was leading and luckily managed to steer through the carnage when he came upon it, said "gracias" and won the race.

TOP: Juan Manuel Fangio came across a track all but blocked by a first-lap accident as he started his second, steered past it and raced on to win in 1950 for Alfa Romeo.

ABOVE LEFT: Graham Hill loved Monaco and won there five times. This is the two-time world champion crossing the finish line for the fifth of these, for Lotus in 1969.

BELOW: The Monaco circuit snakes around the harbour where, during the Grand Prix weekend, hundreds of boats of all shapes and sizes are moored.

PATRESE WINS CRAZY 1982 MONACO GRAND PRIX

If you think that the final lap of the 2008 Brazilian Grand Prix was exciting, as it decided whether Lewis Hamilton or Felipe Massa would become World Champion, it had nothing on the closing laps of the 1982 Monaco Grand Prix. This was the race that no one seemed to want to win. Renault's Alain Prost was in control with 10 laps to go as light drizzle fell. He slowed a little and Brabham's Riccardo Patrese closed in. Then, on lap 74 out of 76, Prost crashed at the chicane. He was out of the race on the spot, and so Patrese found himself heading for his first win, until he spun going into the Loews hairpin and stalled. Didier Pironi assumed the lead, only for his electrics to fail. This meant that Andrea de Cesaris would win, but he ran out of fuel. Then Derek Daly's gearbox seized, and so Patrese, whose car was pushed out of a dangerous position, got going and finally took that win.

The dangers of Monaco were made clear in 1952, when the grand prix was held as a sportscar race and Luigi Fagioli was thrown out of his car. He died three weeks later. Because of the proximity of hard things to hit, bumps that could rattle a car into submission and the fact that someone else's accident could take an innocent driver out, the race has a history of surprise winners. Maurice Trintignant was one such in 1955, when he benefited from Juan Manuel Fangio and Stirling Moss retiring their Mercedes cars and Alberto Ascari crashing his Lancia into the harbour. He escaped unharmed, but this left the way clear for Trintignant to bring his Ferrari from ninth to victory.

There have been some drivers of straightforward genius too, and Stirling Moss's run in 1961 was one of the most notable as he outran the superior "Sharknose" Ferraris in his Rob Walker Lotus. Graham Hill knew just how hard to attack and won five times between 1963 and 1969, whereas many of his rivals pressed just that little bit too hard. Take Johnny Servoz-Gavin, who burst into the lead in his Matra in 1968 in only his second grand prix, but clipped a barrier, causing driveshaft failure. From hero to zero... Ayrton Senna felt that way too in 1988 when he was leading but hit the barriers at Portier and disappeared to sulk.

Just a year earlier, Lorenzo Bandini also pushed too hard, giving chase rather than trying to escape in the lead. He clipped the chicane and was trapped under his burning Ferrari, later succumbing to his injuries.

One of the most spectacular accidents occurred in 1980 when Derek Daly took a shortcut to reach the first corner, Ste Devote, bouncing his Tyrrell off Bruno Giacomelli's Alfa Romeo, flying over Alain Prost's McLaren and landing on Jean-Pierre Jarier, his own team-mate...

One thing that has always added an extra twist to Monaco has been the arrival of rain. It had been wet from the start in 1984, and Nigel Mansell passed Prost for the lead after the Frenchman had had to lift as he went past Corrado Fabi's Brabham facing the wrong way in the tunnel... This was the first time Mansell had led a grand prix and he rocketed away at two seconds per lap, but lost control on a road marking and thumped the barriers on the climb towards Massenet... The later stages of that race were enlivened as Prost was hunted down by Ayrton Senna's Toleman which, in turn, was being caught by Stefan Bellof's Tyrrell. The clerk of the course saved Prost by stopping the race early, just as Senna prepared to pass.

Changes are rare at Monaco, but the biggest improvement came in 2004 when the pit lane was rerouted and larger pit garages built facing the harbour. Monaco will always have a special place on the calendar.

ABOVE LEFT: The upgrade of the pits in 2004 finally gave the teams some space in which to operate.

ABOVE: An official pass giving access to both the grid and the pitlane is more sought after at Monaco than at any other circuit in the world.

ENCLOSURE: A brochure for Fairmont Hotel. As well as being one of the world's most exclusive hotels, it's unique in that the circuit runs under it.

THE 1990s
MASTERCLASSES OF SENNA AND SCHUMACHER

As the cost of Formula One rocketed, so did its spectacle, with grand prix greats Ayrton Senna and Michael Schumacher producing masterful drives that put their rivals in the shade.

The 1990s started with Ayrton Senna versus Alain Prost and came to a close with Michael Schumacher versus Mika Hakkinen, while in between there was also fantastic racing, albeit clouded by a double disaster in 1994. At the San Marino Grand Prix first Roland Ratzenberger died in qualifying, then Senna in the race. It was a catalyst for a change in attitude to driver safety.

Prost started the decade as reigning world champion, but Senna wanted revenge. The only difference for 1990 was that Prost was no longer his McLaren team-mate but now racing for Ferrari instead. At least this made it easier to spot who was who when they got close, and this made it simple to identify the culprit at the Japanese Grand Prix when Senna pushed Prost's red car off at the first corner. It was blatant, yet it earned him his second world title.

The biggest change for 1991 was the resurgence of Williams, with Nigel Mansell and Riccardo Patrese dominating the second half of the season, but Senna's flying start, winning the first four races, was enough for him to be world champion again.

The most promising rookie performance that year came at the Belgian Grand Prix, when Michael Schumacher stepped in at Jordan, substituting for Bertrand Gachot who had been jailed for assaulting a taxi driver. Had Gachot kept his cool, Michael might never have been given the chance to get his foot in the door...

Then came 1992, and Nigel Mansell dominated in a way that few have dominated before. Eight wins in the first 10 races in his Williams-Renault was remarkable, and it was hard to equate this with the driver who didn't win until his sixth season in the sport's top category. The title was wrapped up with five races still to run, and his score was almost double that of the next driver, his team-mate Riccardo Patrese.

Such was his dominance that many expected a repeat in 1993, but Williams had decided to replace him with Prost, who also won as he pleased. However, his return to competition clearly reinvigorated Senna, and the Brazilian produced one of the greatest drives in Formula One history in the European Grand Prix at Donington Park. Rebuilt and reopened in 1977 by Tom Wheatcroft, the circuit now had its day of days as Senna fluffed his start from fourth on the grid. He dropped to fifth but then, on a wet track, simply picked off each of the four ahead of him, the last of them being Prost, whom he simply humiliated that day.

It was Senna's turn to dominate for Williams after a change of teams for 1994, but he failed to win the first two races. They went instead to Michael Schumacher, who was going ever better for Benetton. Then came the ill-fated San Marino Grand Prix. Rubens Barrichello was lucky not to be killed on the Friday, then Ratzenberger crashed fatally in qualifying. In the race J.J. Lehto stalled and was hit by the last car away, Pedro Lamy's Lotus, which shed wheels into a grandstand, injuring a spectator. Then Senna crashed to his death. Finally, in the pits Michele Alboreto's Minardi lost a wheel, which struck several mechanics. It was awful and unbelievable.

With Senna gone, it was left to Damon Hill to rally the Williams team, and he came so close to

ABOVE: Ayrton Senna found himself being pushed very hard by Jean Alesi's Tyrrell in the opening race of 1990 around the streets of Phoenix.

BELOW: David Coulthard's McLaren race suit displays the team's attention to detail and his pride in being a Scot by bearing the saltire. Fireproof driving gloves offer comfort and protection.

LEFT: Damon Hill wore a modern version of his father Graham's helmet design and became the first second-generation world champion, in 1996.

BELOW LEFT: Nigel Mansell comes under pressure from Ayrton Senna in the McLaren, left, and Benetton's Michael Schumacher in the 1992 Brazilian GP, but he made it three wins from three and went on to win the world title.

MIKA HAKKINEN

Every now and again, a driver who is out-and-out fast hits the scene. Mika was one such driver. After taking the British Formula Three title at his second attempt, he vaulted straight to Formula One with Lotus in 1991, running with the big names on his debut at Phoenix. In 1992, he peaked with fourth in Hungary, before signing for McLaren for 1993, banking on Ayrton Senna retiring. But Senna decided to race on, and Mika only got to race when Michael Andretti returned to Indycars. Mika immediately outqualified Senna, and in 1994 raced to second in Belgium. Despite suffering head injuries in Australia in 1995, Mika shone in 1996 before taking his first win at Jerez in 1997. It all came right in 1998, a year in which he won eight times to beat Michael Schumacher to the title. Champion again in 1999 (below), Mika opted for a sabbatical in 2002 but never returned.

taking the drivers' title for them, but was taken out by Schumacher in the final round, which gave the German the title.

Schumacher was able to make it two titles on the trot in 1995, but this time it was more clear-cut. He was helped in no small part by Benetton getting its hands on Renault engines.

Hill then made a little history in 1996 by becoming the first second-generation Formula One driver to become champion, but he had to resist the challenge of his Williams team-mate Jacques Villeneuve, another son of a famous father. His reward? To be dropped by the team...

Schumacher had had a building year at Ferrari in 1996, but he was back at the front in 1997. However, although great credit was due to him for the way he and team boss Jean Todt had turned Ferrari around, he deserved none for the reprehensible lunge he made to try to prevent Villeneuve overtaking him at the Jerez finale. It didn't work, and Villeneuve was happy to throttle back and let Mika Hakkinen take his first win for McLaren, as he'd done enough to be champion.

In 1998, it went to the wire again, but Schumacher chose the worst time to stall before the parade lap and had to start from the back of the grid in the final race of the season, which meant that the title went to Hakkinen.

The Finnish driver did it again in 1999, but Ferrari's challenge had been left in Eddie Irvine's hands after Schumacher broke a leg at Silverstone. The German was back by the time Formula One made its first visit to Sepang, in Malaysia, and by holding Hakkinen back he allowed Irvine to win and give himself a title shot at the final race in Suzuka. There, however, Hakkinen was in total control, with Irvine coming home a distant third.

ABOVE: Michael Schumacher celebrates his 1997 win in Japan, but his title challenge would come unstuck in the final round, losing out to Jacques Villeneuve.

BELOW: Mika Hakkinen's 1997 McLaren-Mercedes MP4/12, with the silver and black West livery replacing the long-standing red and white of Marlboro.

ENCLOSURE: Cigarette cards were particularly popular in the 1930s, but they lived on into the 1990s and this Formula One promotional set was issued by Castella.

AYRTON SENNA
MERCURIAL GENIUS

Intense, moody, spectacular, even a genius ... just a few of the words most often used to describe this much-fêted Brazilian. On his day, no one could get near him, and then came Imola 1994...

yrton Senna won three world championships. A magnificent achievement in its own right, it becomes greater with the realization that his cars were not always the class of the field. It seemed certain that his arrival at Williams would bring many more titles, but he died three races into his contract on 1 May 1994.

Since racing began, there have been a handful of drivers who have stood clear of the rest, who have been feared by the others or expected to win. There was Tazio Nuvolari in the 1930s, Juan Manuel Fangio in the 1950s, Jim Clark in the 1960s, Senna in the 1980s and Michael Schumacher at the start of the 21st century. Sometimes their margin of superiority wasn't huge, but it was still there, along with a sort of inevitability that they would come out on top, just like Tiger Woods in golf and Manchester United in football. It's all about having the right mind-set to deliver the winning performance, about expecting to win. Ayrton wasn't in it to make friends; he was in it to win.

Ayrton collected national karting titles at will. Then at 21, it was time to go car racing and he moved to Britain to compete in Formula Ford, following the example taken by his compatriot Emerson Fittipaldi. Ayrton was a winner by only his third race in 1981 and he went on to be champion, but there was doubt as to whether he would return to Europe. He did, deciding that he was prepared to put his privileged life in São Paulo on hold. British and European Formula Ford 2000 titles followed, and then Ayrton and Martin Brundle had a prodigious battle for the 1983 British Formula Three crown. Ayrton won the title at the final round

ABOVE: Ayrton Senna's helmet design sported the yellow, green and blue of the Brazilian flag and has been much copied by aspiring racers.

BELOW: Senna and the McLaren-Honda MP4/4 was a dream pairing, producing eight race wins and his first world title in 1988.

TOP: Senna scythed his way up the order to finish second at Monaco for Toleman in his debut season in 1984. Had the race not been stopped early, he might have won.

ABOVE: Starring in the wet again, Senna drove took his Lotus 97T to his first Formula One win at Estoril in 1985. Team boss Peter Warr, right, greets him.

and, with it, tests with McLaren and Williams. Both were impressed, but neither offered him a ride, and so Ayrton signed for Toleman for 1984.

Most people conjure images of McLaren when they think of Ayrton, but to a few it was what he did in a Toleman that etched the most profound memories, because of his ability to hurry the car along far faster than it ought to have been going. His second place, in the wet, at Monaco, where he was catching Alain Prost just as the race was stopped, was magnificent, but his third place at Brands Hatch was equally praiseworthy.

It was clear that a win wouldn't be long in coming, and his move to Lotus for 1985 produced this. On only their second race together, in the streaming wet at Estoril, Ayrton won by more than a minute. A run of five podium finishes, including a win at Spa-Francorchamps, helped him rank fourth. He also proved his exceptional ability to knit together a qualifying lap, as his seven pole positions proved. Team-mate Elio de Angelis managed just one.

Ayrton showed his self-interest and his persuasive powers when he convinced Lotus not to sign Derek Warwick for 1986, reasoning that the team had enough trouble already preparing one car to last a race, and that

trying to do so for two high-calibre drivers would be a disaster. A change to Honda engines boosted Ayrton to third in 1987, and he took the first of his six wins at Monaco, but he wanted more and moved to McLaren for 1988, just as the team changed to using Honda engines.

The relationship started beautifully, as Ayrton won eight races and became World Champion. However, this was only after an increasingly bitter battle with team-mate Prost. This battle didn't abate in 1989 or 1990 and, denied a second world title when Prost took him off in the Japanese Grand Prix, he returned the "compliment" 12 months later when he drove Prost off the track at Suzuka's first corner.

Fortunately, Prost was no threat in 1991, and Ayrton instead had to contend with Nigel Mansell and a resurgent Williams team, but his seven-win tally was enough for his third world title.

For 1992, Williams was mightier still, and there was little that Ayrton could do to stop Mansell, except where it was tight and

twisty: Monaco and the Hungaroring. Having to run with Ford engines in 1993 gave Ayrton little chance as Prost took over at Williams, but he still won four times, his opening lap drive at Donington Park being the work of a genius. His final two wins, in Japan and Australia, elevated Ayrton past Damon Hill to be runner-up as he prepared to move to Williams, loving the fact that Prost would quit instead of staying to try to match him.

Thus the way was clear for the creation of what many saw as the ultimate partnership: Ayrton, Williams and Renault engines. However, he had a new challenger in Benetton's Michael Schumacher, who won the opening two races. And then came Imola. Ayrton was on pole, but feeling unsettled by Roland Ratzenberger's death the day before. Formula One doctor Professor Watkins had advised him that he was too upset to start. But start he did, and he was leading when the field was released after a safety car deployment, but speared off and hit the wall at Tamburello. Not only was this a double disaster after Ratzenberger's death, but it removed the fastest driver of his generation.

ABOVE: Ayrton Senna's race suit, boots and gloves rest on a suitably patriotic background as his exploits empowered even the poorest Brazilians.

ABOVE LEFT: Ayrton Senna celebrates what turned out to be his final victory at the 1993 Australian GP ahead of Alain Prost and Damon Hill.

RIGHT: Williams signed Senna for 1994. He leads Michael Schumacher, Gerhard Berger, Damon Hill and Heinz-Harald Frentzen in the third round at Imola, but the race would claim his life.

SENNA WINS THE 1991 BRAZILIAN GRAND PRIX

The wins started flowing in 1985, but it took until 1991 for Ayrton Senna finally to win on home ground. There had been two world titles already with McLaren, but he really wanted this race win and so did his home city crowd. His record at Interlagos thus far was second place in 1986 and third in 1990, the remaining five races having resulted in four retirements and one disqualification. Ayrton qualified on pole – but then he'd done that three times there before. This time was different. A glance at the lap chart shows that he led every lap, but it was no stroll in the park, as Nigel Mansell hounded him until his gearbox failed. Senna's gearbox was playing up too and he had to jam it in sixth for the final lap, slithering on a recently dampened track as Riccardo Patrese drew closer in the second Williams. At the end, exhausted, Ayrton had to be lifted from his car.

McLAREN
TECHNICAL EXCELLENCE

Bruce McLaren was a racer/engineer extraordinaire, whose team lived on after his death and is now the gold standard, also branching out into road car production.

ABOVE: A set of mechanic's overalls, complete with the fireproof boots, gloves and helmet for use during a pitstop with refuelling.

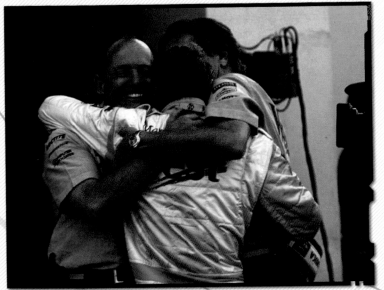

Bruce McLaren didn't live long enough to enjoy the fruits of the team bearing his name. Team McLaren began racing in 1966, but Bruce, himself a four-time grand prix winner, died in a testing accident in 1970 before it became one of Formula One's heavyweights.

The first thing that you need to understand about Bruce is that he, like his late 1950s Cooper team-mate Jack Brabham, cut his teeth racing Down Under. The will was there, but spare parts weren't. Bruce's make-do-and-mend skills, combined with his engineering studies, gave him a considerable start on his European contemporaries in understanding the machinery they raced. In fact, Bruce was the ultimate engineer/racer, as happy in the garage as on the track.

Already with three grand prix wins from his days with Cooper, the first of which was achieved at a then record 22 years and three months, McLaren's thoughts turned to going it alone as Cooper's form slid. He'd already formed Bruce McLaren Motor Racing to field a pair of cars in the Tasman Cup series in New Zealand and Australia at the start of 1964, winning the New Zealand Grand Prix and two other races to be champion. This was the start of an outfit that would evolve into a grand prix team that made its debut in Formula One at the 1966 Monaco Grand Prix. Its initial focus, however, was on sportscars, and this became the rock on which the team was founded when they went on to dominate the lucrative North American CanAm series.

The chief problem for its first grand prix car, the M2B, was the lack of a decent engine. Bruce opted for a scaled-down Ford Indycar V8, hoping that this would bring finance from the blue oval marque. It didn't, and the engine was not only heavy but short on horsepower, so after just one race Bruce decided to fit a Serenissima V8 instead. This offered even less power but was lighter, and Bruce scored McLaren's first point with it on its second outing.

MCLAREN'S FIRST WIN, AT SPA 1968

Jack Brabham had made history in 1966 by becoming the first driver to win a grand prix in a car bearing his name, but Bruce became the only other driver to do so, at the 1968 Belgian Grand Prix. He had a good record at Spa-Francorchamps, having finished second three times, and he'd shown winning form in the non-championship Race of Champions at Brands Hatch, but this hadn't translated itself into points in the Spanish or Monaco Grands Prix. Bruce qualified sixth and Chris Amon led away, but his Ferrari's radiator was holed by a stone. Then John Surtees led Jackie Stewart and Bruce's number two, Denny Hulme, until his Honda's suspension collapsed. Hulme retired when a driveshaft went and so Stewart's Matra had the race under control. When Bruce crossed the finish line, he was happy with second place, only to discover that Stewart had had to pit for fuel and so victory was his.

TOP: Team founder Bruce McLaren put his eponymous team on the map when he contested the 1966 Monaco GP with his own car, the Ford-engined M2B.

LEFT: Ron Dennis (left) and Mansour Ojjeh embrace Mika Hakkinen (back to camera) after he had clinched the drivers' title at Suzuka in 1998.

The availability of the Ford DFV engine to teams other than Lotus for 1968 was a turning-point for his team, as this was a real step-up from the BRM and Weslake engines McLaren tried in 1967. Mated with the M7A, it gave Bruce his first competitive grand prix car, and their third outing together brought victory in Belgium (see sidebar). With a revenue stream coming from winning five straight CanAm titles, and compatriot Denny Hulme proving a winning driver, the course was set fair. But then Bruce was killed testing a CanAm car at Goodwood in 1970.

Teddy Mayer took over and guided the team to the drivers' and constructors' titles in 1974 with Emerson Fittipaldi, and then James Hunt to the drivers' title in 1976. However, the run of wins from 1972 came to an end in 1978, Hunt and Patrick Tambay failing to get in among the winners as McLaren failed to master ground effects. One felt that, had Bruce still been around, they would have.

The team changed course when Ron Dennis took over in 1980, initially in partnership with Mayer. Soon the team was solely his, and John Barnard's groundbreaking MP4 helped it back to winning ways when John Watson won the 1981 British Grand Prix. When Niki Lauda returned from retirement in 1982, the team won four times, but its big bang was in 1984 when Lauda and Alain Prost won 12 grands prix between them to land McLaren its second constructors' title. Five more titles followed up to 1991, with 1988 exceptional for the fact that Prost and Ayrton Senna won 15 of the season's 16 grands prix.

McLaren also set new standards in presentation. It was fastidious in every aspect, and if that made the team seem overly corporate, it merely masked the passion within. It was this driving force that attracted Mercedes to become a partner in 1995. They took a while to gel, but Mika Hakkinen raced to titles in 1998 and 1999, ably supported by David Coulthard.

Since then, however, there has not been a constructors' title as Ferrari has dominated, but McLaren is back at its best, and the arrival of Lewis Hamilton, a driver it has mentored from his karting days, coincided with the team becoming once again a match for Ferrari. An espionage charge in 2007 was an unwelcome distraction, and McLaren had all of its points annulled, but it bounced back to guide Hamilton to the 2008 drivers' title, although that much sought-after constructors' title remained out of reach. The all-British pairing of Hamilton with Jenson Button from 2010 has brought plenty of race wins but, as yet, no titles.

Bruce would have been thrilled by what McLaren has achieved, but the thing that he would have found hardest to imagine was its progress from the old Colnbrook base at the end of Heathrow's runways to its two modern bases in Woking and, most of all, to its current headquarters, the stunning McLaren Technology Centre. That McLaren also makes road-going supercars for Mercedes and does work for other manufacturers would have delighted him even more, especially as its grand atrium retains a link right the way back to the Austin special that he used to race around his garden in Auckland.

BELOW: A selection of McLaren's most successful cars are kept in the MTC's foyer to emphasize the team's illustrious history.

BOTTOM: Ayrton Senna drove this McLaren-Ford MP4/8 to mesmerizing effect to win the 1993 European GP in tricky conditions at Donington Park.

MICHAEL SCHUMACHER
THE RECORD BREAKER

Being fast in a Formula One car is one thing, but Michael brought much more than that. His determination and desire took him to another level, as seven titles attest.

Michael Schumacher shattered every leading Formula One record: seven world titles, 91 wins, 154 podiums, 1,369 points in 16 seasons. Brilliant in the wet, and ruthless in any conditions, Michael dominated as no other: in 2002 he was on the podium at all 17 races, and in 2004 he amassed 148 points, winning 13 times.

The eternal debate about who is the best driver ever will rage and rage, but in fact it's impossible to compare drivers from different eras. If today's drivers were transported back to the 1960s they would have to learn to step back from the edge in their quest for speed and overtaking. In those days cars broke more often, and tracks were considerably more dangerous if you overstepped the mark. But Schumacher is certainly in the top bracket.

Having a father who ran a kart circuit set Michael on the road to the top, as he developed the speed and balance that marked him out as one to watch as soon as he reached car racing in 1988. Advancing to Formula Three in 1989, he was pipped to the title, but won it at his second attempt. The fact that there were no Formula One rides open for 1991 was perhaps the making of Michael, as he was kept on in his parallel sportscar programme with Mercedes, in which young German drivers were placed under the tutelage of more experienced drivers. Michael partnered Jochen Mass and won in Mexico City.

Out of funds for single-seaters, manager Willi Weber landed him a one-off ride in Japanese Formula 3000, and Michael stunned everyone by finishing second in this very competitive category. This put him back in the shop window, and he was Eddie Jordan's pick to replace Bertrand Gachot in his Formula One team when the Belgian was jailed for assaulting a taxi driver. Qualifying seventh made everyone sit up and take notice. Tom Walkinshaw liked what he saw and immediately secured his services for Benetton from the next race, at Monza.

Michael was very sure of his own abilities and he proved them when he won 12 months later at the same venue, Spa-Francorchamps, by combining an ability to press hard in mixed weather conditions with a massive helping of fortune when he spotted that his team-mate

BELOW: Michael's first world drivers' title came his way in 1994, but only after a controversial final race incident with Damon Hill on the streets of Adelaide.

TOP: Michael Schumacher makes his Formula One debut for Jordan in the 1991 Belgian GP, leading Benetton's Robert Moreno, the driver that he would replace at the next race.

LEFT: Unlike his predecessors, Schumacher's helmet design changed throughout his career. He wore this helmet to his first world title in 1994.

ABOVE: Schumacher celebrates his breakthrough Formula One victory, for Benetton, at Spa-Francorchamps in 1992 12 months after his debut there. Incredibly, 90 more wins would follow.

Martin Brundle's tyres were chunking. This helped him rank third overall behind Williams duo Nigel Mansell and Riccardo Patrese.

By 1994, Michael was no longer a confident, occasional grand prix winner but the main man. He won nine times that year, although his Belgian Grand Prix victory was taken away for a technical irregularity. But his battle with Williams's Damon Hill got very heated, and the way in which Michael clinched his first drivers' title at Adelaide doesn't reflect well on him. After Michael had hit a wall and damaged his Benetton, Hill, unaware of this, dived for a gap to take the lead and Michael drove him into the wall to ensure that he, not Hill, would be champion.

A second title followed in 1995, after which Michael accepted the challenge of turning Ferrari back into a championship-winning outfit. He did this in conjunction with the input of Jean Todt, who sorted out the team's organizational side. The tifosi weren't sure of Michael at first, but his win in the wet at Barcelona, by 45 seconds, convinced them.

Michael had his first title shot with Ferrari in 1997, but again he let himself down in the final round when, realizing that title rival Jacques Villeneuve might pass him, he drove across into his Williams. This time, he failed to stop his rival and lost the title. In 1998, however, Michael had a wonderful battle with a driver he considered his equal, Mika Hakkinen and the McLaren pipped him to the crown. Battle was rejoined in 1999, but Michael's season was wrecked when he broke a leg at Silverstone.

This simply delayed the inevitable, and Michael won the drivers' championship for Ferrari in 2000, becoming its first champion since Jody Scheckter in 1979. His 2001 campaign produced nine wins and left him with almost double the points of his closest challenger, Coulthard. It was the same story in 2002, this time with team-mate Rubens Barrichello second best and 67 points behind. Motor racing is cyclical, however, and McLaren hit form again in 2003. Kimi Raikkonen pushed Michael hard, forcing him to use all of his experience to stay ahead, while Juan Pablo Montoya also challenged for Williams.

Thirteen was Michael's victory tally in 2004 as he raced to his final world title, after which he had to face up to a new world order in 2005 when it was Renault and McLaren that had the legs. He won only once and Fernando Alonso stopped his run of titles.

Alonso won again in 2006, but Michael's final season almost brought title number eight. He signed out in Brazil with a drive that showed the very best of his skills. A fuel pump failure left him 10th on the grid, but he rose to fifth, suffered a puncture, then drove from last to fourth, lapping far faster than anyone.

After racing motorbikes for a few years, with limited success, Michael returned to F1 in 2010, this time with Mercedes GP, but top results have eluded him.

ABOVE: Michael Schumacher went out on a high with a magnificent drive from last place to fourth in the 2006 Brazilian GP.

TOP LEFT: Sporting an extremely questionable red wig, Schumacher celebrates his 2000 World Championship title with Ferrari. Rubens Barrichello is behind him, also in a wig, while team principal Jean Todt looks across from the right.

LEFT: Michael shares a joke with Nico Rosberg (left) and team boss Ross Brawn after his return to F1 with Mercedes in 2010.

FERRARI F310

The car that turned Ferrari back into a winning force – at least it did with Michael Schumacher at the wheel – was the F310. Designed by John Barnard for the 1996 season, this was Ferrari's first car without a V12 engine since the V6 turbo-powered F188C of 1987. With its V10 engine behind his shoulders, this was the car with which Michael started his Ferrari career, the car with which he took victory in heavy rain in the Spanish Grand Prix, beating the driver that he'd replaced, Jean Alesi. Further wins followed at the Belgian and, fittingly, Italian Grands Prix, and the tifosi soon adored Michael for turning Ferrari back into a team that could challenge for glory on a regular basis rather than just occasionally. Using a modified version, the F310B, in 1997, Michael fell at the last fence when he clashed with Jacques Villeneuve's Williams as they fought out the world title in the finale at Jerez.

FIA

THE ORGANIZATION OF FORMULA ONE

Battles to be at the head of Formula One haven't been fought only on the tracks. Away from the circuits, the FIA and FOCA have often grappled for control of the sport.

LEFT: Formula One's powerbrokers Bernie Ecclestone (left) and Max Mosley chat back in their relatively carefree days of team ownership.

RIGHT: New FIA president Jean Todt makes a rare appearance at a grand prix with his his wife Michelle Yeoh.

The Fédération Internationale de l'Automobile (FIA) is Formula One's governing body. Headed by Max Mosley, it sets the rules of racing, creates the schedule and decides on venues. However, it must be added that nothing in Formula One happens without the approval of Formula One Management, run by Bernie Ecclestone, which handles its promotion and commercial rights.

Formed in 1904, the FIA is the body to which all 222 national motoring federations are affiliated, and its elected president oversees all motor sport, with the FIA running the top championships in all categories from Formula One to the World Rally Championship.

All officials are bound by this Paris-based, non-profit association's guidelines. The president serves a four-year term and in 2005 the FIA members voted that no president could serve more than two terms. Current president Mosley is approaching the end of his fourth.

The FIA formed an autonomous committee, the CSI (Commission Sportive Internationale), in 1922 to run its motor sport activities as distinct from its bread-and-butter road car element. This later became known as FISA (the Fédération Internationale du Sport Automobile), but that became outmoded in 1993 when motor sport was brought back under the direct control of the FIA, with its World Motor Sports Council governing all FIA-regulated events.

Name changes aside, for as long as there has been motor sport, there have been power struggles about

LEFT: Mercedes-Benz supplies the high-performance safety and medical cars for all the grands prix wherever they are held around the world.

RIGHT: Known as "Bakersville" after chief Eddie Baker, this is Formula One Television's massive production headquarters that is set up at each race.

who runs what. One thing remains clear: it is the FIA that decides the technical regulations that have shaped the sport. If the FIA wants to control costs to keep Formula One safe or healthy in times of economic downturn, then it does so, setting them into a legal framework called the Concorde Agreement that locks them in place for a fixed number of years.

The early 1980s witnessed a power struggle between FISA and the Formula One Constructors' Association (FOCA). Alfa Romeo, Ferrari and Renault sided with FISA, while the British "garagistes" who existed only to race – including Brabham, McLaren and Williams – took FOCA's side. FOCA had grown strong through the 1970s with Brabham supremo Ecclestone at its helm. Indeed, race organizers gave him the prize fund to distribute. FISA boss Jean-Marie Balestre felt compromised, and this led to the FISA teams withdrawing from the 1980 Spanish Grand Prix when the organizer backed FOCA. The race went ahead with 22 cars and was won by Alan Jones for Williams, but it was declared null and void.

The second chapter came at Kyalami at the start of 1981, when FOCA, wanting to force the issue of racing with skirts – for ground effect – which FISA had banned, arranged an extra grand prix. Nineteen cars turned up and Carlos Reutemann won for Williams, but it was to count for nothing. When the FIA-sanctioned World Championship kicked off at Long Beach a month later, the ban on skirts stood.

The final skirmish was at Imola in 1982, where the FOCA teams refused to turn up as two of their drivers had been excluded from first

and second places in Brazil for running underweight thanks to a rule that said that brake coolant could be topped up. This had led the FOCA teams, in their quest to match the turbo cars, to dump their coolant and then have it topped up before post-race scrutineering. Their no-show at Imola left just 14 cars, but this time the race was allowed to count. Matters were never this bad again.

Disregarding the politics, Formula One is run to a tight rulebook, with the cars having to conform to hundreds of regulations, and officials at every race have the role of keeping "creative" designers in line. These are the scrutineers, who check every car any time that they go out on to the track, while cars can also be called to the scrutineering bay at any time at random. This is the garage closest to the pit entrance, in which the FIA's scrutineering rig is located. This is a hydraulic ramp on which the car is weighed and templates are used to check dimensions. Perhaps the most intense scrutiny comes after the race when the cars are gathered in parc fermé – a fenced area into which no team personnel are allowed to encroach.

The overall responsibility for the running of a grand prix falls to the clerk of the course, while there are three race stewards to adjudicate in any appeals that arise, such as on technical eligibility or on driving standards. Recently, the calibre of the stewards has come under scrutiny, with discontent focused on their level of professionalism. Teams felt increasingly that it would be better to have a former driver making the rulings rather than three unpaid individuals who may have little or no experience of the grand prix scene. They got their wish and now the panel of stewards is made up of three ex-drivers, with their selection on a rolling basis. Another change has been the election as president of former Ferrari team principal Jean Todt in place of Max Mosley and he has taken a less high-profile stance and focused more broadly on the entire sport.

BELOW: With security of paramount importance, only personnel with the correct passes issued by Formula One Management are admitted to the paddock, having to pass through electronic security gates to gain access.

BELOW RIGHT: Lewis Hamilton went to a court in Paris in a bid to overturn a ruling that went against him following an incident with Kimi Raikkonen in the 2008 Belgian GP. He failed to have it overturned.

BERNIE ECCLESTONE

Formula One simply wouldn't be what it is today if it wasn't for Bernie. Until the early 1970s, there was a lack of organization in the World Championship, with teams coming and going and the power in the hands of the circuits. The teams felt that they deserved more negotiating strength, and Ecclestone was the one with the commercial acumen to achieve this, getting them together as the Formula One Constructors' Association. After racing motorbikes and then Formula Three, Bernie first became involved with team ownership when he bought a couple of Connaughts in 1957. His next role was managing Jochen Rindt, and after Rindt's death in 1970 he bought Brabham, which he ran until 1986. However, the role for which he is best known is as head of Formula One Management, and he runs the commercial side of the sport to this day, giving Formula One an ever wider global spread.

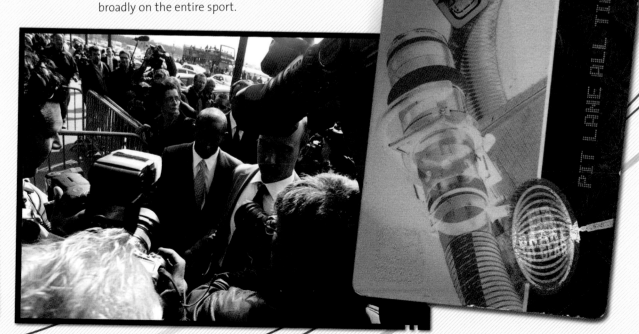

NEW WORLD
GLOBAL EXPANSION OF FORMULA ONE

The days of Formula One being a European sport are long gone. Its tentacles now stretch around the globe, with new races being added, often in place of traditional ones.

ABOVE: China was added to the calendar in 2004, with its Shanghai International Circuit amazing everyone with its gigantic grandstands.

Formula One has staged grands prix on every continent except for the polar ice caps. It is true that Europe was its starting-point and remains its home, and although both Morocco and South Africa have been on the World Championship calendar it has been many years since there was a grand prix in Africa. However, the sport is now expanding into Asia, with Abu Dhabi, Bahrain, Turkey, Singapore, Malaysia and China joining long-time players Japan on the programme, with India, South Korea and Russia in the pipeline as motor racing heritage is replaced by government funding.

This all seems a far cry from when the first World Championship in 1950 consisted of seven rounds, all of which were held in Europe – in Britain, Monaco, Switzerland, Belgium, France and Italy – except for the oddity of the Indianapolis 500 counting as the seventh round, even if no one from Formula One tended to cross the Atlantic Ocean to compete in that or vice versa.

Little changed through the 1950s except that Argentina provided a distant sortie to start the year, Holland and Germany joined in, and then the Swiss government banned racing within its borders after the 1955 Le Mans disaster. A one-off grand prix on Italy's Pescara road course plugged this gap, then Portugal was added in 1958, and Morocco's Ain-Diab circuit outside Casablanca also had a one-off.

Then, two years before the Indy 500 was dropped, the USA was awarded a grand prix in 1958 and this was followed by neighbouring Mexico in 1963 and, four years later, Canada. The US Grand Prix took three years to find a home and, when it left Watkins Glen in 1980, had to do without a fixed venue until it settled on using an infield circuit at the Indianapolis Motor Speedway in 2000. Canada's race was held mainly at Mosport Park until Montreal was inspired to build a circuit, and its timing was perfect as it coincided with the ascent of Gilles Villeneuve. The cost of hosting a grand prix has since proved too much and Canada has dropped from the calendar for 2009, sadly joining the US Grand Prix, which left Indianapolis a year earlier and has yet to find a new home.

Much as Argentina was inspired to have a grand prix from 1953 thanks to the exploits of Juan Manuel Fangio, Brazil joined in from 1973 thanks to Emerson Fittipaldi's triumphs on the world stage. South Africa's grand prix was afforded World Championship status in 1962 and traditionally started the season, but it lost its race in 1986. It regained it for two years from 1992, but has remained on the sidelines since.

Perhaps the most exotic addition came in 1976, when Japan was awarded a grand prix, and nine years later Australia joined in for an end-of-season double-header.

TOP: Formula One's world tour last took in a race in Africa, at Kyalami, South Africa, in 1993. Ayrton Senna leads Alain Prost and Michael Schumacher.

LEFT: Sebastian Vettel leads Nico Rosberg at the start of the 2011 Turkish GP, but it failed to attract the crowds required to ensure its future.

The number of European races was also boosted in the 1980s, with Italy being granted a second race under the convenience title of the San Marino Grand Prix, even though it was run at Imola rather than within borders of the principality. Later, when Michael Schumacher was at his peak, Germany gained a second race, at the Nurburgring, under the convenience title of the European Grand Prix – once it was even the Luxembourg Grand Prix. The new race that broke the most ground came in 1986 when Bernie Ecclestone propelled Formula One behind the Iron Curtain into what was then communist Hungary.

The only new grand prix in Europe in recent years has been on the Valencia street circuit, now carrying the European Grand Prix courtesy title, no doubt as a result of Spain's Fernando Alonso winning two world titles. Just across the border, hoping to put Portugal back on the world championship map, a new world-class circuit has been built in the Algarve.

It should be noted, most especially with the global economy having entered recession, that all is not sweetness and light. The organizers of the Chinese Grand Prix, run on the very expensively tailor-made Shanghai International Circuit, have stated that it may not be able to afford to continue after its contract to host a grand prix runs out in 2010. It might be the first to reverse the trend. Indeed, some future races, such as the ones planned for India and, most especially, Russia, might yet be prey to economics.

For races in Europe, where no government funding is forthcoming, many of the traditional grands prix might follow the French GP onto the sidelines, with the German GP looking shaky, but Silverstone finally secured its future after undergoing modernisation.

Conversely, the USA is back from 2012 with a new circuit at Austin, Texas, following South Korea onto the calendar, with Russia to follow in 2014. However, it's not just the cost of building a circuit to land a grand prix that is proving a problem for countries that want the prestige of a grand prix but then find that they can't fill the grandstands and have to watch their business models unwind. On top of this, Bernie Ecclestone wants the circuits in the Far East to follow Singapore's example and use floodlighting so that races can be run at night and thus go out in daylight hours in Europe to capture the most important TV market.

CIRCUIT DESIGNER HERMANN TILKE

If Bernie Ecclestone has been the dominant figure in Formula One's history, then it's safe to say that Hermann Tilke has also played a major part in shaping the face of Formula One from the late 1990s. Why? Because Tilke is Ecclestone's chosen circuit architect, with his design studio shaping Sepang, Shanghai, Bahrain (below), Istanbul, the Valencia street circuit and most recently Abu Dhabi's Yas Island circuit. His trademark is a tight first corner sequence opening out into a flowing middle section. Tilke also sorted out the modifications to the infield section at Indianapolis, the reshaping of the start of the lap at the Nurburgring and the shortening of Hockenheim, as well as being responsible for the outlines of forthcoming circuits in South Korea and India. This former club racer is the man who has defined the style of racing that the drivers of the day may or may not enjoy.

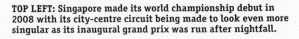

TOP LEFT: Singapore made its world championship debut in 2008 with its city-centre circuit being made to look even more singular as its inaugural grand prix was run after nightfall.

LEFT: Abu Dhabi's Yas Marina circuit set new standards for circuit infrastructure.

THE 2000s
SCHUMACHER DOMINATES, THEN IS REPLACED

Michael Schumacher shattered record after record for Ferrari, but no one can rule for ever, and a whole crop of new drivers is now doing the winning, spicing up Formula One again.

Success doesn't always yield the result you might expect, and Michael Schumacher and Ferrari's astonishing run of success from 2000 came close to ruining the sport. Once people thought that they knew what the outcome would be before each race began, hundreds of thousands of fans were not bothering to watch. Fortunately it forced rival teams to raise their games, and the result has been a spike in interest since they struck back, with hungry young drivers such as Fernando Alonso, Kimi Raikkonen, Felipe Massa and Lewis Hamilton breathing life into the drivers' championship.

Schumacher showed that he meant business in 2000. After being beaten in 1998 and 1999 by McLaren's Mika Hakkinen, three straight wins for the German driver set the tone, but then came wins for McLaren's David Coulthard and Hakkinen, and the teams would swap wins through the year. It looked as though Hakkinen had made a break by winning the Belgian Grand Prix with the passing move of the decade, but Schumacher struck back at Monza, then won the final three to send Ferrari wild with delight.

Schumacher won nine times in 2001, with closest challenger Coulthard winning just twice. At least a third team got in among the trophies, with Williams using BMW engines to help Ralf Schumacher to three wins and Juan Pablo Montoya to one. Hakkinen would later admit that he'd been shaken in the opening race when suspension failure pitched him into the wall, prompting memories of his accident in 1995 when only prompt medical treatment saved him. He bounced back at Silverstone, but had lost so much ground that he could rank only fifth.

ABOVE RIGHT: Fernando Alonso storms clear of the field at the Hungaroring in 2003 on his way to his first win, at 22.

ABOVE: The red and yellow bands on Alonso's helmet signify Spain, the blues to match his Renault's livery in 2005.

BELOW: By leading his McLaren team-mate Fernando Alonso in the opening race of 2007 in Australia, debutant Lewis Hamilton issued a challenge.

ABOVE: Michael Schumacher was the man of the decade, landing five drivers' titles with Ferarri. His best year was in 2002, when won 11 races, including at Suzuka.

It was Schumacher again in 2002, with his tally of 11 wins eclipsing everyone. Even team-mate Rubens Barrichello managed to win four times. Make that five, as he was asked to move over to let Schumacher win the sixth race of the year, in Austria, and did so out of the final corner, just to make it plain what he thought of this. The public weren't happy either, especially as Michael didn't need the help.

Schumacher made it four in a row in 2003, but he was pushed by McLaren's new flying Finn Kimi Raikkonen. The battle went all the way, with Raikkonen going to the final round in Japan with an outside chance, but he needed to win and could manage only second behind Barrichello. Williams had also been in the mix through Montoya, but the Colombian had to settle for third overall.

The first seven races of 2004 produced just one point for Raikkonen and this helped Schumacher, but his chief rival was from team-mate Barrichello, although everyone knew that he would never be allowed to challenge his team leader. Jenson Button continued to help BAR advance and, although he never won, 10 podium finishes left him third.

In 2005, Schumacher was finally deposed by Fernando

JORDAN CHANGES ITS NAME, THREE TIMES

Leopards never change their spots, but teams change their owners and thus their identities. One such team was Jordan, founded by Eddie Jordan from his successful Formula 3000 team in 1991. It was bright, fun and occasionally won, but the cost of trying to take the battle to Ferrari and McLaren became too much, and Jordan had to be sold. This happened at the end of 2004 when Russian industrialist Alex Shnaider bought the assets and renamed the team Midland F1. Perhaps the cost of competing escalated faster than he could invest, but the team's decline continued. It was sold on midway through 2006 to Dutch sportscar company Spyker. That too failed to impress, and the team is now in its fourth incarnation, as Force India, after billionaire Vijay Mallya's purchase before the 2008 season. He then struck a deal to run McLaren's Mercedes engines and gearboxes from 2009, making his intentions clear.

Alonso, who won seven races for Renault. Raikkonen was runner-up as McLaren rediscovered its feet, with Montoya at the wheel of its other car. So great was the swing that Schumacher would rank only third, and even his sole win in the US Grand Prix was a fortunate one. Only six cars took the start, the 14 Michelin-shod cars having driven back into the pits as the French tyre manufacturer couldn't vouch for the safety of its tyres on the banking after a blow-out pitched Ralf Schumacher into the wall.

Schumacher fought back in 2006. Level on points with Alonso with two races to go, he was leading in Japan when his engine failed. Alonso won and the title was all but his. For Schumacher only victory would do in the Brazilian finale, but a failure in qualifying left him 10th, then a puncture dropped him to the back, and although he recovered to fourth, second was enough for Alonso. It was certainly worth noting that Michael's team-mate Felipe Massa was triumphant that day.

With Schumacher retired, the new guard had to set their own levels in 2007, and at the opening grand prix rookie Lewis Hamilton showed that there was another driver capable of mixing it. Racing for McLaren, Hamilton also showed that he was no respecter of reputation, jinking around McLaren's other signing, Alonso. Raikkonen, now with Ferrari, won that first race, but it was Hamilton and Alonso who ranked first and second going to the final round. Hamilton hit trouble again in Brazil and victory for Raikkonen enabled him to pip both, by a point.

Hamilton got his revenge in 2008. Having led for most of the season, he went into the last race at Interlagos needing only a fifth-place finish, and it seemed he had done enough until rain fell late in the race and it became a lottery. Hamilton was passed by the year's revelation Sebastian Vettel and Massa seemed to have grabbed the title as he raced to victory. But, as the Brazilian crossed the line, Hamilton passed Timo Glock, struggling on dry-weather tyres, and the title was his. The story of 2009 was the rise of Brawn GP from the ashes of Honda Racing and the way that Jenson Button scored five wins to lift the title. Then in 2010 it was Vettel's and Red Bull Racing's turn. At 23 years and 106 days, Vettel became the youngest ever world champion.

ABOVE RIGHT: Jenson Button kicked off his incredible 2009 campaign with victory in the Australian GP for the new Brawn GP team.

RIGHT: Sebastian Vettel was another driver to score his first win in 2008, his victory coming in the Italian GP at Monza. At 21 years and 73 days, the German driver became Formula One's youngest ever grand prix winner.

BELOW: The Ferrari F1-2000 was the car driven by Michael Schumacher on his way to the decade's first World Championship. It was Ferrari's first world drivers' title in 21 years.

THE NEW GENERATION
HAMILTON AND VETTEL RISE TO THE TOP

Michael Schumacher's dominance for Ferrari ended in 2004, since when Fernando Alonso, Kimi Raikkonen, Lewis Hamilton, Jenson Button and Sebastian Vettel have all showed their talents.

Change can be good and even Michael Schumacher's most dedicated fans understood that it would make a change for another driver to be World Champion after the German great won five in a row. What they wouldn't have foreseen was that when Renault's Fernando Alonso ended Schumacher's run in 2005, not only would Michael not be crowned World Champion again but also four other drivers would become claim the title over the next five years.

These were Kimi Raikkonen for Ferrari in 2007 – after Alonso had edged out Schumacher to make it two on the trot in 2006 – then Lewis Hamilton for McLaren in 2008, Jenson Button for Brawn GP in 2009 and Sebastian Vettel for Red Bull Racing in 2010. All of a sudden, F1 had a new guard, drivers capable of not just winning grands prix when the opportunity arose but mounting a year-long campaign consistent enough to be

TOP RIGHT: Sebastian Vettel's victory at Valencia in 2011 made it his sixth win from the first eight races of the season. His helmet is shown on the opposite page.

BELOW: Lewis Hamilton cuts the chicane on the opening lap of the 2007 Italian GP at Monza, but he was beaten to the chequered flag by McLaren team-mate Fernando Alonso.

champion. Seldom has F1 enjoyed such variety in the list of drivers becoming the World Champion.

Although Raikkonen quit racing for rallying, Alonso continues to offer an unbelievably competitive spirit, Hamilton is the most attacking in traffic and Button the best in mixed conditions, Vettel appears to have the best mix of talents though, but no little credit should go to Red Bull Racing for supplying him with the best car.

Their merits were then given clear comparison when Schumacher returned to F1 in 2010 with Mercedes GP (successors to Brawn GP) after three years away and struggled to match their pace. Sure, Michael was no longer in the most competitive car as Red Bull Racing, McLaren and Ferrari provided their drivers with faster, better handling machinery. However, there were signs that the seven-time World Champion was no longer the main man, as he made mistakes in traffic and was outpaced frequently by team-mate Nico Rosberg, a driver considered to be right up there in the pack of new stars.

Furthermore, there were other drivers, such as Mark

A TIME OF ACRONYMS

Stating that sports fans should be entertained and not confused seems a simple enough edict. However, while aware of the first part of this and focusing on boosting the amount of overtaking, F1's powerbrokers came close to blundering with the latter. Among the Overtaking Working Group's solutions was the introduction of KERS in 2009. Fans didn't need to understand the inner workings of the Kinetic Energy Release System (it stored energy that would otherwise be lost from heavy braking to offer an extra 80bhp to help with overtaking), but it was used successfully only by McLaren. and was dropped for 2010. KERS was reintroduced for 2011 when it could be used in conjunction with another acronym: DRS – Drag Reduction System. DRS helps a driver to boost his straight-line speed by being allowed to open a slot between the two planes of his rear wing in a controlled zone – usually the main straight – in the hope of producing a passing move.

Webber, who proved when he finally got his hands on a competitive car at Red Bull Racing that he could win races too. If things panned out differently for the Australian, he might have had a run at the 2010 title, although he was made to feel number two to Vettel and, if things broke on their cars, it was almost inevitably his. Then, in 2011, Vettel was able to get more from their car, so Webber's star waned. Felipe Massa, who occasionally outpaced Schumacher when they were team-mates at Ferrari, also deserves mention. Indeed, the Brazilian thought for half a minute after winning the final race of 2008 at Interlagos that he'd become World Champion in front of his home crowd. Then, Hamilton managed to out-sprint Timo Glock, whose Toyota was on dry tyres on a wet track, on the blast to the finish line to take the place he needed to be champion instead.

One driver who has been in the mix is Robert Kubica, winning in a BMW Sauber then shining for Renault. His rivals, many of whom raced him in F3, feared the day that he would land a ride with a top team. But then he suffered a dreadful arm injury when competing in a rally at the start of 2011, costing him his F1 season as he recovered. Whether he'll ever be as quick on his return will have to be seen; sadly, very few drivers manage it after a

major injury. But Robert was one driver that the hot shots like Hamilton and Vettel feared for his outright speed and near faultless delivery.

Now, on the evidence of the 2011 World Championship, even these new stars are going to have to watch their tails as the next crop of drivers are snapping at their heels. Japan has waited a long time to have a top driver, but Kamui Kobayashi could be that man. After some startlingly effective drives for Toyota at the end of 2009, he proved one of the great entertainers in 2010, with a never-say-die attitude to overtaking, even though he was in only a mid-grid Sauber.

Kobayashi's team-mate in 2011, Mexican rookie Sergio Perez, also showed considerable maturity, mastering long runs on worn tyres that more experienced rivals normally avoid in the hope of achieving better finishes. Jaime Alguersuari, the youngest driver ever to start a grand prix – he was 19 years and 125 days old when racing at the 2009 Hungarian GP – has also shown flashes of brilliance for Scuderia Toro Rosso.

Leading the charge among the latest rookies, though, is Paul di Resta. Despite beating Vettel to the 2006 European F3 crown, the Scotsman could not keep his single-seater career going and was placed in touring cars by Mercedes. Di Resta was DTM runner-up at his second attempt and then champion in 2010 before Mercedes eased his passage into F1 with the Mercedes-powered Force India team. The speed was there and a ride with a top team will surely follow. All the rookies have to hope, though, that they end up in the right place at the right time.

ABOVE: The Renault team helped Fernando Alonso to win the first of his two world championships in 2005 ahead of Kimi Raikkonen.

BELOW: Jenson Button takes the chequered flag at the 2011 Hungarian GP after another intelligent victory in mixed conditions.

BOTTOM LEFT: Red Bull founder Dietrich Mateschitz's money transformed the team and turned Mark Webber into a grand prix winner.

PUBLISHING CREDITS

First published in 2009
Second edition 2012

Copyright © Carlton Books Limited 2009, 2012

A CIP catalogue record for this book is available from the British Library.

Carlton Books Limited
20 Mortimer Street
London W1T 3JW

ISBN: 978-1-84732-992-9

Editor: Martin Corteel
Art and design direction: Darren Jordan
Designer: Katie Baxendale, Luke Griffin
Additional design: Stefan Morris
Photography: Karl Adamson
Picture research: Paul Langan
Production: Rachel Burgess, Maria Petalidou

Printed in China

CREDITS

The publishers would like to thank the following sources for their kind permission to reproduce the pictures in this book:

Carlton Books: /Karl Adamson: 1, 8r, 9b, 11br, 12l, 12r, 17b, 18t, 18bl, 19br, 20r, 22tr, 23c, 24tl, 26c, 27b, 30l, 31b, 32c, 33tr, 33br, 35t, 38t, 39b, 40l, 43tl, 43c, 43b, 44l, 45b, 47r, 48c, 48br, 49b, 50l, 51tr, 52l, 53b, 54l, 57r, 60l, 61b

Getty Images: /Michael Cooper: 29tl, 41br; /Keystone: 38bl; /Jean-Pierre Muller/AFP: 41bl; /Paul Popper/Popperfoto: 25bl; /Popperfoto: 25tr; /Mark Thompson: 39r

LAT Photographic: 6t, 6bl, 6r, 7tl, 7tr, 7b, 8t, 8l, 8br, 9l, 9r, 10tl, 10tr, 10br, 11tr, 11bl, 12t, 12rt, 12rb, 13b, 14r, 14bl, 15tl, 15r, 15b, 16tl, 16tr, 16br, 17tr, 17l, 17r, 18tl, 18tr, 18br, 19l, 19tr, 20t, 20bl, 20br, 22tl, 22br, 23tr, 23bl, 24t, 24r, 24bl, 25br, 26t, 26bl, 26br, 27tl, 27tr, 27r, 28t, 28bl, 28br, 29br, 30tr, 30bl, 30br, 31tr, 32tr, 32b, 32br, 33tl, 33c, 34l, 34tr, 34br, 35l, 35br, 36l, 36t, 36br, 37l, 37br, 38l, 38br, 40t, 40bl, 40br, 41tr, 42tl, 42tr, 42bl, 42br, 43tr, 43r, 44tr, 44bl, 44br, 45r, 46l, 46tr, 47c, 48tr, 48bl, 49tr, 50tr, 50r, 50b, 51br, 52tr, 52bl, 52br, 54tr, 54r, 54b, 55br, 56t, 58t; /Charles Coates: 29bl, 39l, 55tr, 56l, 57tl, 60t, 60bl; /Glenn Dunbar: 4-5, 21b, 45tl, 55bl, 62t, 62bl; / Steve Etherington: 35r, 37r, 47tl, 51l, 55l, 58l, 59tl, 59bl, 59r, 60r; /FOTA: 53r; /Robert Fellows: 13t, 13c, 14t; / Andrew Ferraro: 61r, 63bl, 63br; /Gavin Lawrence: 61l; /Jean Michel Le Meur/DPPI: 57b; /Colin Mcmaster: 21l; /Motor: 33l; /Red Bull Racing: 63tl; /Tony Smythe: 23br; /Steven Tee: 46b, 56Br, 61tr, 62br, 63tr

Press Association Images: /Michael Steele/Empics Sport: 49l

Topfoto.co.uk: /AP: 31l

(Abbreviations: t-top, b-bottom, l-left, r-right, c-centre)
Every effort has been made to acknowledge correctly and contact the source and/copyright holder of each picture, and Carlton Books Limited apologises for any unintentional errors or omissions, which will be corrected in future editions of this book.

All the facsimile memorabilia in this book was sourced from the Donington Park Collection, with the following exceptions:

Belgian Grand Prix postcards (pages 8–9) – courtesy of the Musée de la Ville d'Eaux, Spa, Belgium;

Mercedes obituary notices (pages 12–13) – courtesy of Daimler AG;

Maserati and Vanwall contracts (pages 24–25) – courtesy of Sir Stirling Moss;

Brian Hatton and Dick Ellis cut-away drawings (pages 26–27) – courtesy of Haymarket Consumer Media;

Hotel brochure (pages 46–47) – courtesy of Fairmont Monte Carlo.

The publishers would like to thank Kevin Wheatcroft, Neil Leavesley, Garry Rankin and David Peacock for their unstinting efforts in making available the cars, helmets and other items of F1 memorabilia from the motor museum at Donington Park that are reproduced in this book.

TRANSLATIONS

Page 13, enclosures 3 and 4: Two Mercedes-Benz obituary notices, for Dick Seaman who crashed to his death when leading the 1939 Belgian Grand Prix at Spa-Francorchamps.

OBITUARY

The outstanding sportsman, our friend, the highly esteemed and very popular racing driver

JOHN RICHARD BEATTIE SEAMAN

died tonight, at the age of 26, from injuries resulting from a serious accident which occurred during the Belgian Grand Prix.

The deceased was already a well-known personality in the world of motor sport when he became a member of our racing team in 1937. Thanks to his excellent driving skills, he soon earned a place among the highest class of racing drivers. He had many successes – we need mention only his victory in the 1938 German Grand Prix and the splendid race he drove in the 1937 Vanderbilt Cup Race in the U.S.A., in which he came second. Even in the Belgian Grand Prix, which was to be the last race in which he took part, he demonstrated his great ability and his masterly control of his fast racing car. However, he went off the track on a bend which had become very slippery due to heavy rainfall. Although he was given medical attention immediately, and it initially appeared that the young driver's life would be saved, Seaman succumbed to his severe injuries shortly before midnight.

In John Richard Beattie Seaman, we have lost a great driver and an exemplary human being. He will be mourned by his family, by the wife he married a few short months ago, and by his friends in the sport. He will be equally missed by the management and workers of our company. In him we have lost an outstanding and promising competitor and a very good friend. We honour his memory, and he will not be forgotten.
Stuttgart-Untertürkheim, 26th June, 1939

The management and workers, Daimler-Benz Ltd.

DAIMLER-BENZ LIMITED LIABILITY COMPANY
STUTTGART-UNTERTÜRKHEIM HEAD OFFICE

Works newsletter no. 371
to all main and subsidiary sales offices, main agencies, agencies, sales outlets, distributors and contract workshops in Germany and abroad.
Our ref.:
Publications Department BW/EM
26th June, 1939

Re.: Belgian Grand Prix

Mercedes-Benz win again in Belgian Grand Prix
But the 5th victory of the year comes at a high price: Richard Seaman in fatal accident

Yesterday, after a hard and dramatic struggle, Mercedes Benz won their fifth consecutive great victory of the year when their ace driver, Hermann Lang, came first in the Belgian Grand Prix. Thanks to a long period of heavy rain, the difficult and fast sections of the Spa-Francorchamps track had become quite extraordinarily dangerous. This meant that, from the beginning of the race onwards, the most extreme demands were made on racing cars' engines, brakes and roadholding, and also on the drivers' abilities. And so it was no surprise that there was an extraordinarily high number of incidents of every kind during this race.

Our four Mercedes-Benz drivers, Rudolf Caracciola, Manfred von Brauchitsch, Hermann Lang and Richard Seaman demonstrated their great abilities as world-class ace drivers. But Caracciola had to withdraw from the race on the eighth lap, when his car spun round on the narrow, slippery track and the engine refused to restart. However, the other drivers continued to drive an excellent race. Hermann Lang came first and Manfred von Brauchitsch was placed third. Dick Seaman drove with great style. He was only sixth in the first lap but, in spite of the fact that the track was like glass due to the continuous rain, he managed to move up into the lead. He held this position from the eleventh lap onwards, surrendering the lead for one lap only when he had to make a pit stop to refuel. That's how things were right up to the twenty-third lap. But he met a tragic fate in the twenty-fourth. He left the track at the shallow Francorchamps bend. The car spun round, as Seaman could no longer correct the fault, due to the very narrow track. It went backwards into a tree. The car caught fire and Richard Seaman himself had to be carried off the track, severely injured. Although the medics were on the scene straight away, and everything possible was done to save the young driver's life, John Richard Beattie Seaman succumbed to his grave injuries shortly before midnight. With his death, we lose a great driver and an exemplary sportsman.

A dark cloud thus overshadows Mercedes-Benz's splendid new victory. In Richard Seaman, the management and workers of Daimler-Benz have lost a competitor of the first rank. All our employees will forever honour his memory, and he will not be forgotten.
Please find enclosed for your information a press release which relates to the race itself. In the circumstances, we shall not be distributing a race poster at present. However, we shall send you one within about 10 – 14 days, as it will still be of topical interest.

Daimler-Benz Limited Liability Company

Page 19, enclosure 1: Letter and a telegram sent and received by Tazio Nuvolari in 1951. Upon his return to racing after the War, he was 54 and suffering from ill-health.

Mantova, 4.10.51

Dear Sperti,
As agreed at our last meeting in Pescara, please send me a small collection of wool fabrics for women's and men's autumn clothes, at your discretion, including some in grey. Also enclose some samples to make a lady's jacket. I am in bed with the flu after my trip to Naples and Foggia.
Add a few samples for a lady's coat. I look forward to hearing from you.
With kind regards,
....

Via Rimembranze 1, Mantova

Form C. – Tel 63						Form 30 – (1951)
URGENCY	Received on...... 19....... Time.......					The time is calculated from the meridian, corresponding to the mean time in Central Europe. In telegrams printed in Roman letters, the first number after the name of the place of origin represents that of the telegram, the second that of the words, and the others the date, hour and minutes of presentation.
Position	DESTINATION PESCARA	ORIGIN	NUMBER	WORDS	DATE OF PRESENTATION	For office use
					Day and month / Hour and minutes	

(8201037) Ord. 15 – Rome, 24.7.1951 – 1st. Poligr. Stato P.V. (e. 32,000,000)

27 PESCARA DA MANTOVA 9800 18 10 12/10+

ON MY RETURN FROM ROME I FOUND A MAGNIFICENT DINNER SUIT – IT WILL BE A SUMMER FAVOURITE. THANK YOU. KIND REGARDS – TAZIO NUVOLARI +

Page 25, enclosure 3: The invoice for preparing the 1954 Maserati 250F to race in British Racing Green. In those days a car's colour depended on the nationality of the driver.

MASERATI
OFFICINE ALFIERI MASERATI
LIMITED COMPANY – REGISTERED OFFICE IN BOLOGNA – CAPITAL OF 50,000,000 LIRE PAID-UP

Mr STIRLING MOSS
20 William IV Street
Charing Cross
LONDON WC2
(England)

P.O. Box 170

ADMINISTRATIVE OFFICE AND
WORKS IN MODENA
VIALE CIRO MENOTTI, 322
Tel. 24-262 – 23-451
Telegrams: MASERATI

Post Office Account: 8-4209
Modena Chamber of Commerce: 36756
Bologna Chamber of Commerce: 64644
Code: ABC – 6.a Ediz.

Balance/Account	Your order	Our acceptance	Shipping	Invoice date
				14/1/1954

Re: PROFORMA INVOICE
Goods delivered: ex-works in Modena   Packing

Shipping address and method:

Payment: opening of irrevocable letter of credit at the Italian Commercial Bank in Modena, payable on presentation of delivery or shipping documents.

1	Maserati 250/F Formula 1 Racing Car – new, single-seater chassis painted British Racing Green with a red stripe around the radiator grill, complete with no. 4 wheels with tyres and tool kit. Extras: 4 spare, bare front wheels 4 spare, bare back wheels 4 spare axle ratios for the price of.....................£ sterling	3,561.00